Transfiguring Time

Understanding Time in the Light of the Orthodox Tradition

Published in the United States by New City Press
202 Comforter Blvd.,
Hyde Park, NY 12538
www.newcitypress.com
©2019 English Translation, Jeremy N. Ingpen

Translated by Jeremy N. Ingpen from the original
French edition *Transfigurer le Temps*, Delachaux
& Niestlé, Paris, 1959
©Monique Clément

Cover design and layout by Miguel Tejerina

Transfiguring Time
Library of Congress Control Number:
2018962568

ISBN 978-1-56548-680-5 (paperback)
ISBN 978-1-56548-681-2 (e-book)

Printed in the United States of America

Transfiguring Time

Understanding Time in the Light of the Orthodox Tradition

by
Olivier Clément

Preface by
Ilia Delio, OSF

Translated by
Jeremy N. Ingpen

New City Press
Hyde Park, New York

"*In this insightful and definitive translation of* Transfigurer Le Temps, *Jeremy Ingpen introduces the English-speaking readership to the wonderfully complex world of Olivier Clément. One of the greats of the Paris theological school, Clément was a prolific and revered French lay theologian, who published some thirty books and a hundred articles devoted to theology, history, and spirituality of the Orthodox Church. In Ingpen's translation, Clément is revealed as a thinker of a great openness of mind, someone who understands well the problems of modernity and post-modernity. A powerful voice for Orthodoxy in France, whose messages resonated far beyond France and Europe, Clément labored within the intellectual tradition laid down by his mentor Vladimir Lossky. In one of his earlier works,* Transfiguring Time, *Clément explores the working of the Holy Spirit in the world, and outlines his vision of transformational Christianity, a tradition deeply rooted in Patristic thought. Combining readability with a wealth of thoughtful insight, this translation will prove indispensable to those seeking a solid understanding of Olivier Clément's theological and philosophical thought.*"

Lasha Tchantouridzé, PhD,
Professor of Church History, St. Arseny Orthodox Christian
Theological Institute, Winnipeg, MB, Canada; Deacon, St. Jacob
of Alaska Orthodox Church, Northfield Falls, Vermont

"*Jeremy Ingpen's translation of Olivier Clément's* Transfigurer le Temps *is an important contribution to our modern understanding of the theological/metaphysical dimensions of time and being. Clément's views, solidly grounded in the thought of the early Church Fathers, and rightly including a background of classical references, are all the more impressive for his study of time and eternity in the context of other religious perspectives; Buddhist and Hindu thought are covered in quite some detail. Besides reviving this virtually forgotten French text, this translation reveals its importance as a profound meditation on religious history in general. The question of time and its relation to the meaning and understanding of Christi-*

anity, and that of space and the temporal dimension relative to the transcendental, remains one of the greatest mysteries confronting the human mind. Even in this day of quantum mechanics, information theory, and practical physics, scientific descriptions of time still elude concrete determination. Clément's unique approach reviews and unravels the threads of the Christian transfiguration of time in and beyond the purely temporal domain and should therefore be of utmost interest and concern to a wide range of thoughtful readers. With gratitude we applaud this presentation of this significant theological work, at last available in the English language."

Rodney Purcell Devenish,
Buddhist Meditation instructor and founder of Kunzang Samten
Yangtse Hermitage, Denman Island, Canada

Contents

Preface

On April 6, 1922, a significant conversation took place between the leading philosopher of the day, Henri Bergson, and the renowned physicist, Albert Einstein.

It was a momentous occasion and one that would ultimately affect how we understand the nature of time. The debate was charged with vehemently opposing views: Einstein claimed that time was simply physical and psychological while Bergson claimed that Einstein's theory of time prevented us from realizing that "the future is in reality open, unpredictable, and indeterminate."[1] Bergson was so adamant in his position that his authority on the matter influenced the Nobel Prize committee who, in fact, did not give the Nobel Prize to Einstein for his work on relativity but for his work on the photoelectric effect. "Thanks to Bergson," Jimena Canales writes, "we now know that to act on the future one needs to start by changing the past."[2]

This is precisely the point Oliver Clément makes in *Transfiguring Time*. Instead of a scientific or philosophical approach to the question of time, Clément pursues this fascinating dimension of reality from the point of religion. Unlike the cyclic religions of birth, death, and new life, the author looks to the particular way Christianity makes sense of time as eternity inserted into history. He asks, "How can that which is always present come into the world?" Whereas theologians usually ponder how eternal being can become something other than eternal being, such as in the Incarnation, Clément asks how the eternal God can enter into time and become dependent on time. The Incarnation is a time-dependent event, the mystery of the "acceptable time," the *kairos* prepared by the Eternal God and enacted by the Word made flesh. Time and matter are bound up together, which ren-

---

1. Jimena Canales, "This Philosopher Helped Ensure There Was No Nobel for Relativity," *Nautilus*, April 21, 2016, 4.
2. Ibid., 1.

ders time more than a physical dimension of light, as Bergson realized; eternity is enmeshed with time so that there is a simultaneity of time and eternity at every moment. The cosmos is intrinsically temporal in such a way that time is part and parcel of nature's creativity. In the perpetual transition from non-being to being, the created is embedded in change and temporality so that the future is integral to nature's becoming or, better yet, nature's transformation.

The Incarnation breaks open this profound reality of time and discloses the future of the material world as the capacity for radical transformation in God. Time, therefore, is not an innocent bystander to space, a mere measurement of change; rather, time is the most intimate dimension of personhood, both individual and cosmic personhood; it is the rhythm and fundamental polarity of creation.

Clément draws on the richness of the Christian tradition to show the depth and breadth of time as the most fundamental aspect of the God-world relationship. By doing so, he illuminates a metaphysical depth to time that is missing from scientific descriptions of time and space. Rather than simply being a dimension of space relative to the speed of light, time is the dimension of creativity and change that is inextricably linked to the revelation of personhood and love. The destiny of the cosmos is entwined with time so that just as the cosmos is oriented toward fulfillment in God, so too time is oriented toward fulfillment in eternity. Clément writes beautifully of this fulfillment as freedom from the barrenness of winter, from suffering and death, for God will wipe away all tears and heal the wounds of the fragile heart. Eternity does not swallow up and dissolve the personal; rather eternity is the transformation of the personal into the full flowering of life, the continuing encounter face to face with the Living God, who is ever newness in Love.

Ilia Delio, OSF
Villanova University

Translator's Introduction

"Within Time, O Mother of God, thou hast borne for us Him who shone forth timelessly from the Father"[3]

The great French Orthodox theologian Olivier Clément was born in the village of Aniane, in the Languedoc region of southern France, to a non-religious family. "I grew up in an environment in which Christianity played no part. I was not baptized and received no religious instruction." Attracted first by poetry, especially that of Rainer Maria Rilke, and then by the Bible, he spent his twenties exploring the religious traditions of India. "For ten years I searched through this vast world of religions and myths. I was drawn to all of it. But I found myself trapped between the spirit of India, where all is sacred, divine, and immersed in the ocean of divinity, and my sense of the uniqueness of the human person."[4]

It was Clément's encounter with Vladimir Lossky's *The Mystical Theology of the Eastern Church* that showed him another way. Lossky's chapters on the Trinity and man made in God's image thrilled Clément. The Trinity appeared to hold the solution to the impasse: "a total unity, greater by far than that spoken of in India, and completely different." At the same time he began to read the great Russian writers, including Dostoevsky and Berdyaev. "I discovered Christianity and I asked myself what I should do with this discovery."[5] Baptized as an Orthodox Christian in November of 1952, Clément went on to study with Lossky in Paris, while teaching history at the Lycée Louis-le-Grand. Clément was invited by Paul Evdokimov

---

3. Matins for 4th Sunday of Lent.
4. Both quotations: Interview with La Croix, 2001, cited by Nicolas Sénèze, "Olivier Clément, grand penseur orthodoxe du Xxe siècle, est mort," La Croix, January 16, 2009.
5. Both quotations: ibid.

to join the faculty of the Institut Saint-Serge in Paris, where he taught for over thirty years.

His first book, *Transfigurer Le Temps: Notes sur le Temps à la Lumière de la Tradition Orthodoxe*, was written when he was 37. It carries all the excitement of his fresh encounter with Orthodoxy and the Fathers of the Christian Church. He draws on his deep study of Hinduism, Buddhism, and Indian myths to differentiate the conception of time and eternity in archaic religions, in Hinduism, and in Buddhism, from the Christian and specifically Orthodox understanding of time and eternity. The print run was very small and the book disappeared from view, almost without a trace. It was referenced only occasionally.[6] This translation will bring Clément's early work to a new generation of readers.

The copy used by the translator belonged to the late George Florovsky and sat unopened for many years on the shelves of St. Vladimir's Seminary Library. Florovsky clearly read it attentively, as his many markings and underlinings indicate. The 1959 publication was in a series entitled Collection de Taizé. In the next five years, Clément published *L'Eglise Orthodoxe*, an introduction to the Orthodox Church, as well as *L'Essor du Christianisme Orientale* and *Byzance et le Christianisme*. *L'Eglise Orthodoxe* has remained in print, while the other two books were reissued in 2009 and 2012. The publication of *Transfiguring Time* in English now allows readers access to all four of Clément's early works.

According to Monique Clément, the author's widow, *Transfiguring Time* is a bridge between Clément's research in the years before his baptism and his immersion in the Orthodox faith. It is also a meditation on history. Because of his training as a historian, the historical approach was central to Clément's way of thinking. These reflections on the "sense of history" contribute to one of the main currents of post-war French thought.[7]

Clément's language is not easy to translate. He uses dense poetical symbolism and a highly rhetorical sentence structure.

6. *Transfigurer le Temps* received a favorable notice from Yves Congar, Revue des Sciences Religieuses, 1961, vol. 35.
7. Monique Clément, personal communication, 2017.

His text resonates with biblical imagery and with the language of the Orthodox hymns and troparia of the Feasts, that rich treasury of poetic religious meditation contained in the Orthodox service books and in the Lenten Triodion.

Clément's analysis speaks to us directly of time and eternity and of the attraction of the escape from the world offered by Eastern religions. To quote Clément's own Introduction: "in our time there are more and more seekers after the 'flight from time' among those who are not simply stricken with metaphysical blindness." In addition to providing an extensive analysis of the conception of time and eternity in archaic religions, Greek philosophy, and Eastern religions, *Transfiguring Time* stands on its own as a meditation on the meaning of time and eternity, rooted in both the patristic tradition and in the newness and shock of Clément's encounter with Christianity. It is also one of the few Orthodox meditations on the Book of Revelation, a neglected text in Orthodox theology.

I have aimed for consistency of terminology and style. In most cases I have translated *le temps* as "time," as opposed to *la temporalité*, which I have translated as "temporal existence." *Le devenir*, which Larousse defines as "the movement by which things transform themselves," with an important and specific usage in Eastern religion, I have translated as the "unfolding present." I have been assisted in normalizing the vocabulary of Hindu and Buddhist religion and of the antique Greek philosophers by Rodney Devenish's thoughtful reading of an early version of the text.

For assistance with specifically Orthodox terminology, I have referred to the classic translations of the Festal Menaion and the Lenten Triodion by Archimandrite (now Archbishop) Kallistos Ware and Mother Mary, and also to the definitive translation of the Philokalia by Archimandrite Kallistos Ware, G.E.H. Palmer, and Philip Sherrard. I have however retained the Biblical "void" of Genesis 1:2 in preference to the liturgical "nothingness" (as in "He brought us from nothingness into being") where Clément discusses that which was before time. The "void" seems to me to avoid the dry existential philosophical connotations of "nothingness." I have tried to be economical with capitalization.

I have capitalized when referring to the Persons of the Trinity. I have capitalized the Bible and also Paradise, when it refers to the Paradise of Genesis. By contrast, other gods and other paradises are in lower case. The distinction between God and gods at least has the merit of consistency with Miles Coverdale's translation of the Psalms in Cranmer's *Book of Common Prayer*, the classic text of the Psalms in the English language.

Old Testament Bible quotations are taken from *The New Oxford Annotated Bible, Revised Standard Version*. New Testament quotations, unless otherwise noted, are taken from Richmond Lattimore's masterful translations.[8] Lattimore stays very close to the original Greek and his translations are closer to the feel of Segond's French translation cited by Clément.[9] Quotations from the Fathers are translated from the French. In most cases I have referenced only the title. Clément's French text contains a full bibliographic apparatus for those scholars who wish to see the quotations in the original language. Where Clément's readings differ from the English translations, I have tried to convey the text as cited by Clément.

Clément mostly avoids the sort of theological language that is impenetrable to the layman. I have however footnoted those terms, such as "economy," that have a specific theological meaning that differs greatly from their everyday usage. For the French *parousie* (*Parousia*), I have in most cases used the more colloquial "Second Coming." Clément's very specific usage of *entasis,* as opposed to *ekstasis*, is defined in a footnote on its first occurrence. In places, Clément's text carries echoes of a polemical debate with the Swiss theologian, Oscar Cullmann, whose *Christ and Time* had recently been published. Perhaps these passages originated as a book review. I have taken the liberty of skipping over some of those polemics, while leaving the core of the dialogue with Cullmann. In referring to the early religions of mankind, I have kept Clément's term "archaic religion" as opposed to the more culturally loaded

8. The Gospels and the Book of Revelation, 1979 and Acts and the Letters of the Apostle, 1982, Farrar, Strauss, Giroux, NY.
9. Louis Segond, La Sainte Bible.

"primitive religion." Clément refers throughout to mankind and man. In many instances I have broadened man to "person" and have used a collective "they" in place of the singular "he."

My thanks to Monique Clément, Michel Stavrou, and his wife Sophie Clément-Stavrou for their blessing of this translation of Olivier Clément's early work. Monique Clément provided valuable biographical details and corrections to previously obtained information. My thanks also to my grandfather, who began to teach me the French language at an early age, and to teachers and friends at the University of Bordeaux and the Institut Saint-Serge, Paris. Many thanks to the libraries of SUNY New Paltz and St. Vladimir's Seminary, Crestwood, New York, which provided a welcoming work environment. Many friends and colleagues have helped along the way. The errors, however, are my own.

Jeremy N. Ingpen
Hartsdale, NY
February 2018

Abbreviations and
Frequently Referenced Sources

Cullmann: Oscar Cullmann, *Christ et le Temps*, Paris, Delachaux, 1947

Lossky: Vladimir Lossky, *The Mystical Theology of the Orthodox Church*, Crestwood, NY, 1969

Eliade 1: Mircea Eliade, *Le Mythe de l'Eternal Retour*, Paris, 1949

Eliade 2: Mircea Eliade, *Traité d'Histoire des Religions*, Paris, 1949

PL: *Patrologia Latina*, Migne

PG: *Patrologia Graeca*, Migne

SC: *Sources Chrétiennes*, Paris

Early Christian Writings: 2nd Ed., Penguin, 1975

The Lenten Triodion: translated by Mother Mary and Archimandrite Kallistos Ware, Faber, 1978

The Festal Menaion: translated by Mother Mary and Archimandrite Kallistos Ware, Faber, 1977

Petite Philocalie: Petite Philocalie de la Prière du Coeur, Paris, 1953

RSV: The New Oxford Annotated Bible, Revised Standard Version, Oxford University Press, 1962

The Four Gospels and the Revelation: newly translated from the Greek by Richmond Lattimore, NY, 1979

Acts and Letters of the Apostles: newly translated from the Greek by Richmond Lattimore, NY, 1982

BCP: The Book of Common Prayer, Church of England, 1662

Introduction

Do not fear. I am the first and the last; I am he who lives.[10]

The value that Western thought places on the history of humankind and on personal history is intimately tied to the "monotheistic" revelation of the Bible, even if this link is no longer a conscious one. In the "monotheistic" revelation the absolute is unveiled in the person of God, who creates other persons in order to summon them toward their deification.

The whole problem of the conceptualization of time is implicitly Judeo-Christian in its origin. The modern myth of progress is a naïve secularized form of the biblical expectation of the Messiah. As Sergei Bulgakov so well demonstrated, the Hegelian dialectic, inherited by Marxism, is merely a degraded form of Trinitarian theology.[11] The philosophers' insistence on the importance of personal history and experience may be traced back through Kierkegaard, Luther, and St. Augustine to St. Paul's conception of faith.

However, to the extent that these concepts have been severed from their theological roots, they have become ungrounded. Therefore it is not surprising to see a resurgence of cyclical conceptions of culture, primarily influenced by the natural sciences, from Nietzsche's "eternal return" to the closed cultural cycles of Oswald Spengler. Such concepts have received additional support in our day from the deeper study of non-Christian Eastern thought, which appears to many Westerners to provide a much more satisfactory account than the Bible for the fabulous dimensions of the universe and time, as revealed to us by modern science, astronomy, and geology.

The vastness of the eons comes as a shock to our system and fills us with anxiety. This is the same anxiety that seized

---

10. Revelation 1:17
11. *The Tragedy of Philosophy*, Darmstadt, 1927 (German translation).

Pascal when Galileo exploded the closed universe of the philosophers of antiquity. This anxiety resembles the Hindu "terror of time"; so much so in fact that in our time there are more and more seekers after the "flight from time" among those who are not simply stricken with metaphysical blindness.

Since Novalis and William Blake, Western literature has been filled with a nostalgia for paradise akin to that of ancient times. This tendency was strengthened in the twentieth century by the study of ancient religions. The pursuit of practices that achieve an escape from time and the poetic magic of *wonderland*[12] converge into a new atheism, that one might call a gnostic or mystical atheism, which poses the most formidable challenge to Christianity in the second half of the twentieth century. It is necessary for Orthodox Christians to define and deepen their conception of time in the face of this new gnosis and of the growth of neo-Christian theologies that present "Christianity on steroids." Unfortunately, Catholic thought, through its doctrine of "dogmatic development," seems to me to have become skewed by the modern myth of the inevitability of evolution, while Protestant thought risks excessive scriptural literalism.[13]

Eternity can no more be reduced to a linear time of indefinite duration, than God can be reduced to the anthropomorphic portrayals of the Bible. Orthodox theology must try to reconcile these opposing values by illuminating personal history with the values of liberty and love that are represented in Dasein philosophy (philosophies of existence) and by illuminating the history of mankind with its true value. Human history is the construction of the kingdom of God; and eternity, in its glorious fullness—that of the sea joined to the sun (Rimbaud)—is a cosmic transfiguration, sought nostalgically by the mystics who proclaim "the end of time" and by the poets of *wonderland*. For too long already the best of humanity has been torn between the crucified Christ and all that Christianity has become silent to, to all that Nietzsche named Dionysism. But should not we, as Christians, rather than

---

12. Translator's note: italics in original.
13. Cullmann, *Christ and Time*.

Nietzsche, the prophet of the eternal return, proclaim in him whom the Apocalypse calls the Amen: *Eternal Yes of Being, I am eternally your Yes, For I love you, O Eternity.*[14]

---

14. Nietzsche, *Lieder des Prinzen Vogelfrei - Ruhm und Ewigkeit.*

Part One

Cyclical Time

*O Destiny, you preceded all the gods
you were readied before all creation;
faithful only to yourself
you are the nakedness of the first origin,
a form that enters everywhere,
cold destiny, both creator and creation,
uniting event, knowledge and awareness.*

*You mask everything in your fearsome revelation -
god descends as a crystal fleece that dissolves into thread
in the empty dome of the dream.*[15]

The non-biblical religions, which, following Père Daniélou, we shall call "cosmic" religions, have a sense of time that is radically opposed to that of modern man. They are animated by a nostalgia for paradise that leads them to consider history as a fall, preventing the return to the original condition, a return to the paradise that dwells on the other side of the material world, or rather, that is the obverse of the material world and of time.

Nevertheless, there is ambivalence about the meaning of the passage of time. For the archaic community, cyclical repetition is the means of a return to paradise. For the individual ascetic of the advanced cultures in which myth has given way to rational systematization, the passage of time becomes, by contrast, the sign of hell itself. In the archaic conception of time, time is

---

15. Hermann Broch, *The Death of Virgil*, 1945.

consumed and regenerated through the common feast, through liturgy. In the rational-ascetic conception of time, time is transcended by gnosis. The first conception leads to the orgy, the second to intellectual disembodiment, or *entasis*.[16]

---

16. *Entasis*: disembodiment or absorption into eternity

1. The Archaic Conception: Repetition as the Return to Paradise

For primitive society, authentic time is the dawning moment of creation. At that moment of grandeur of the origins of time, heaven was still very close to earth and one axis of the world—tree, ladder, or mountain—allowed free passage from one world to the other. This first blessedness, often represented symbolically by the flight of birds, disappeared as the result of a fall, of a cataclysm that separated heaven from earth. In the state of paradise man could meet the gods and speak the language of the animals. Thereafter he was isolated from the divine and from the cosmos.[17]

The whole effort of archaic man was therefore to seek an end to his fallen state in order to be once again in paradise. For paradise has not disappeared completely. It is hidden. It is not reduced to that original instant from which fallen time takes us ever further away: it is also a *state* that is masked by time and that can be rediscovered. All the same there is a fundamental stumbling block. Since the passage of time and the victory of death cannot in reality be abolished, the return to paradise cannot in reality be achieved. The never-satisfied nostalgia of archaic religion therefore leads, on the one hand, to an imitation of the life of paradise that confers on certain privileged moments the taste of escape from a fallen world: and on the other hand it leads to a systematic obliteration of the passing moment through rites of purification and regeneration, an obliteration of that time that is indeed separation and death but which is also innovation and history.

In the original heroic time—the time of the paradisaical moment—the cosmos was organized and the rules of ordered behavior were revealed to mankind by the gods, by the ancestors, or by the heroes. The organization of the cosmos and the revelation of culture continue in secret, underlying and supporting both

---

17. Translator's note: *cosmos* in Orthodox iconography represents that old harmony of the natural world that was disrupted by the Fall and that is restored at Pentecost.

cosmic and social life. Thus the paradise of divine acts is changed
into a heaven of archetypes that lends its cohesion and its ontological density to the universe and to human action. In this view,
reality is for mankind *a repetition of archetypes*, that in one and
the same movement is the restoration of the paradisaical moment
and the unveiling of an eternal present.

"We must do as the gods did at the beginning";[18] "as the
gods act, so does mankind."[19] Marriage and work only make sense
insofar as they repeat the original union of the heaven and the
earth. "I am the heaven, you are the earth," says the Hindu spouse
to his bride.[20] For the Dogons, the inner meaning of a weaving
is to reproduce one of the forms of the original revelation of the
Logos. Every creation (construction) repeats the creation of the
cosmos and attempts to restore the world on its axis. Every sacrifice recapitulates and to some extent coincides with the original
sacrifice—the dismembering of cosmic Logos.

Through ritual—and every human activity becomes ritual-
ized—mankind attempts to participate through recapitulation in
the paradisaical fullness of the archetype. Profane time is destroyed,
or willed to destruction. But time continues. Therefore it is necessary to consume it periodically, or at least to mime its destruction.

That is the meaning of the new year rituals: they destroy
the old year and recreate the world through a return to its origins.
Purging and purification, chasing away demons, the sacrifice of
a scapegoat, all represent the destruction of the "old year," which
is sometimes burned in effigy. The extinguishing of the flame
symbolizes the return to original chaos: the relighting symbolizes
the restoration of the universe. Likewise, carnival rites and orgies
represent a return to the youth-giving fecundity of chaos. Masks
and mummery provide a support to the souls of the dead who
come to pay a visit to the living, since in this interval between two
seasons communication between the seen and the unseen again
becomes possible.

18. *Catapatha Brahmana I*
19. *Taittiriya Brahmana I*
20. *Atharva Veda*, XIV.

Consequently events in history, events that are not part of this cycle of repetition, are abolished. That is to say, history, the breaking forth of an absolute newness that cannot be repeated, and that is embedded in the uniqueness of the human person, is abolished. However, if the personal dimension of time is nullified, the cosmic dimension is not. It becomes the sacrament of eternity. Through this annual rhythm, eternity seems to unite itself to time in order to renew time. The span of human existence finds its meaning in making preparation for the feast, in making ripe that privileged instant in which mankind takes part in the universal return to the center of existence. Archaic thought does not distinguish between human destiny and the destiny of the universe. The rituals of the feast are not a celebration of nature: they are a celebration of the luminosity of the archetypal forms seen through the prism of universal time. They are the rhythms of a universe that has no other substance than to be the symbol of the invisible, a multiform theophany.

The cosmos with its splendid rhythms of day and night, of the lunar cycle, of the calendar year, appears to be a grand liturgy in which each return, of dawn, of the new moon, of the solstice, of spring, affirms the beneficent and ontologically nurturing presence of eternity—the creative union of time and eternity as in the paradisaical moment. The grain germinates, the sun goes beneath the horizon, the moon is reborn, as eternity takes possession of time past and regenerates it, regenerating in the same movement the life of mankind, if only one can know how to unite oneself to the miracle.

The cosmos, in all its parts, waxes and wanes to wax again, following the rhythm of life and death, of evolution and involution, as symbolized by the double helix. Death, in an unformed expectation of rebirth, is understood as return to the primordial, maternal waters, as is shown by the innumerable prehistoric tombs in which the corpse is laid with the knees drawn up to the chin, in the fetal position. There is no immanentism, no adoration of nature for its own sake in this religious intuition, not at least in the most ancient of religious conceptions. For primitive man regularity does not imply inevitability: the rising of the sun, for example, or the winter solstice, the emergence of light in the darkness, are always experienced as a new breaking in of the transcendent, as an act of intervention that is not *owed* but freely granted, and that therefore demands gratitude. In this regard it should be noted that the cycles most revered by primitive humanity were not those of the sun, whose regularity might in the end be taken as a sign of an autonomous existence, but instead the phases of the moon, whose irregularity bears witness to a freely creative divine will.

One important symbol (and ritual), the dance, sums up this conception of time. According to a very ancient tantric expression, the cosmos is the "game of god," the divine dance. Primitive cyclical time is nothing less than the rhythm of this dance, the ever-tighter circle of the spiral or labyrinth around a static axis to which the dancer is drawn in and assimilated. At the limit all movement ceases and time is absorbed into the simultaneity of space, into the omnipresence of the center of eternity suddenly experienced in the instant of creativity. Such is the symbolism of the Vedic altar that encapsulates time and merges it into an immobile representation of eternity. "The altar of fire is the year; nights stand for the stones of the enclosure and there are 360 of these just as there are 360 nights in the year; the days are the bricks and there are 360 of them just as there are 360 days in the year."[21]

The altar not only stands at the center of the world but also at the birthplace of time. The construction of the altar recapitulates the birth of the universe. The water in which the clay is mixed symbolizes the primordial water; the clay of the foundation symbolizes the earth; the partitions symbolize the atmosphere, etc. At Malikula the labyrinthine dances converge around a vertical stone that is both the center of the world and the origin of time.[22] However, mankind cannot achieve immobility at this paradisaical center. History cannot be abolished. The fecundity of the cosmic rhythms leads only to death. That is why the cosmic dance, according to a hymn to Shiva, has a tragic, nocturnal char-

---

21. *Catapatha Brahmana X*, cited by Eliade 1, p. 123.
22. John Layard, Eranos-Jahrbuch.

acter: *"your gardens are graveyards, vampires shape your heart, the ashes of the pyre are your sandalwood perfume, a chain of human skulls is your garland of flowers."*[23]

At Eleusis, a repository of the most ancient symbols, we find not only the mother, Demeter, and the daughter, the virgin Coré (Persephone), but also a third goddess, or rather a third aspect of the same mystery: Hecate, goddess of the terrors of the night and of death. The child Brimos, who is hailed with the words "the great goddess has given birth to a holy infant," did not in reality triumph over death. And "the grain harvested in silence" only sprouted in order to nourish the endless cycle of generation and corruption. And so the rhythms of cosmic time become a nightmare that mankind seeks to escape.

Rural cultures sought refuge in the impersonality of the orgy and in intense orgiastic cults that attempt to deny creation itself and to achieve a sort of interpersonal fusion that is beyond form and law. In place of nature revealed as theophany, as the revelation of divine creation, they substitute an opaque cosmic consciousness, exemplified by the radical autonomy of Pan, the great earth deity. Rather than investing nature with personal deities these worshipers abandon themselves to the intoxication of Eros and to an ecstatic frenzy by means of which they hope to be freed from responsibility (for history) and from the finiteness of diurnal life. Through the orgy and through the altar prostitutes the worshipers regress from the status of person to that of cellular being, as one grain in the undifferentiated primordial chaos seeking to return to the bliss of life in the womb of the great earth mother.

For advanced cultures, the counterparts of the Dionysian exaltation, in which the person is swallowed up in the *meonic* abyss, are the ascetic devaluing of the unfolding present and the search for a different form of saving impersonality, that of the intellect that is beyond cyclical time experienced as a symbol of hell.[24]

---

23. R. Grousset, Bilan de l'Histoire.
24. Translator's note: *meon*, relative nothingness; as opposed to *ouk on*, absolute nothingness.

2.   Systematization and the Ascetic Concept: Repetition as a Sign of Hell

High cultures systematize and to some extent rationalize the two fundamental intuitions of archaic religion: the absence of any barrier between time and eternity in paradise, and the experience of the diurnal and annual rhythms as a participation in the primal all-in-all. This systematization and rationalization leads to an understanding of history as fall, in which the future is always experienced as degradation and forgetting. This is true notwithstanding the counter-concept of the cyclical nature of time, which can be construed as imparting value to the future.

There are two systematic approaches that are of particular interest: that of Western antiquity and that of India. The first posed grave problems for the Christian thinkers of the first centuries; the second made clear, with incomparable lucidity, the metaphysical significance of cyclical time. Ancient Greece had been aware of the cyclical conception of time since the days of the pre-Socratic philosophers. This was the legacy that the myths conveyed to the infant period of philosophy. For example, for Anaximander all things are born of and return to the *apeiron*. The very embodiment, in wounding the original unity, causes matter to be degraded and therefore precarious and unstable. For Empedoclus, cosmic "love" and "hate" create and destroy the universe. Heraclitus evokes periodic conflagrations—the Heraclitean fire. The Pythagoreans taught the eternal return and, in all probability, reincarnation. In his *Politics*, Plato compares the universe to a mobile, built like a model of the heavenly spheres. It is set in motion by the hand of destiny who applies a steady twisting force to the cord from which it is suspended, and then lets go. The cord unwinds and the celestial apparatus spins in the reverse direction. Thus destiny makes the universe alternate perpetually between order and the disorder of abandonment. This disorder is, one should note, fruitful: the process of aging is reversed; the old man becomes a child again; everything is reborn.

In the Greek epoch the theme of cyclical repetition was popularized by the Pythagorean renaissance and by Stoicism, which in turn were influenced by Babylonian astronomy, as transmitted by Berose the Chaldean. The cycles took the form of a succession of grand years, each concluding in an inferno of destruction followed by renewal (*apocatastasis*). Greek thought provided a superb explanation of cyclical time. The fullness of being is an *in-itself (en-soi)*, a stable, immutable eternity, a world of transcendent, primordial archetypes. The unfolding present (*devenir*) belongs to the lower degrees of reality, to the world of sensory perception, which emanates from eternity via a hierarchy of "states of being." The lower levels draw their life and their intelligibility from the higher levels, and assimilate to the higher levels through contemplation, just as the thing of beauty leads to and assimilates to the ideal of supreme beauty.

But at the same time the lower forms degrade the higher forms because they are reflected onto the otherness of the matter that cannot be grasped, according to Plato, except through "bastard" concepts. Time is at once real and unreal, both externality and participation in eternity. When viewed as a linear passage from sameness to otherness, time is inconstancy and mask. But as circular movement (*kyklphoria*) time turns around the immovable center, drawing out and making apparent its force field. Thus time becomes the intelligible rhythm that has its part in the fullness of eternity. Plato demonstrates the divine *Chronos*, the cyclical movement of the supreme heaven, a living and ordered reflection of an intelligible eternity and the mobile image of an immobile perfection. *Chronos* determines the cycles of the stars and these in their turn determine cosmic time, with its alternate phases of generation and degradation.

"*The stars in their return bring back the conjunctures of time past.*"[25] History is therefore no more than a process of cyclical return, in which no event is unique. This is true whether history is understood as an "eternal return" of all possible permutations of human existence, as for Aristotle, or as the transplanting of the

---

25. Synesius the Cyrene, cited from Lacombrade, 1951, p. 116.

human soul into a new body, a condensation of the same cyclical inevitability, as is held by Greek thought. Time is always experienced as a degradation. This is a characteristic of the cyclical return. It is a marker of the persistence of the primitive archetypes of original time and the moment of creation in the depths of the conscious mind. The cycle is always regressive. Time is experienced as a process of inevitable degradation. If everything in intelligible space has been given for all eternity, from the very instant of emanation, as Anaximander stressed, the unfolding present begins to move ever further from its origin. Time is a process of ontological exhaustion. And therefore an *apocatastasis*, a return to the origin, a massive injection of eternity, becomes necessary for the cycle to recommence.

In Greek mythology (as for example in Hesiod) this conception of decay is expressed by the succession of the four ages of humanity: the Golden Age, the Silver Age, the Bronze Age, and the Iron Age. The Greek philosophy of history simply transposed this schema onto the political arena, making history the study of the inevitable decay of an original constitutional purity. Starting from a mythical royal city, Plato unfolds the dramatic succession of aristocracy (government by the best), timocracy (where wisdom gives way to power), and oligarchy (in which wealth triumphs). A fatal revolution then establishes democracy, which quickly degrades into anarchy and the process is resolved into tyranny, the rule of a single tyrant. Plato's thought was formed in the fires of the political life and history of his city. With the ascent of Stoicism, in the context of the depoliticized unity of the Roman Empire, the cosmic vision reasserted its power, together with the cyclical fatalism of *ekpyrosis*, the consumption of the whole world in flames.

Greek thought always showed a special reverence for this world of universal order in which everything has its place, as in a well-ordered choir. We may well speak here of a "cosmic religion." For the *Corpus Hermeticum*, a careful synthesis of pagan religion, the universe is a second god, the "son of god," the cosmic Logos, shot through with divine energy. In order to free himself from the unfolding present, the contemplative should assimilate himself to the cosmic Logos, passing from its rhythmical perpetuity into eternity.

Through the mediation of the cosmos, the contemplative surpasses the cosmos itself to attain an impersonal deity. However, an increasing level of anxiety arises with the opposing force of the astrologers and mathematicians, whose work defines the paths of the stars and the planets, and with the diminution of the role of the city gods, with whom the faithful had been able to bind themselves to the sacred on a personal I-thou basis. Athens's love of fatalism had shown its ambiguous side ever since the classical epoch of the fifth and fourth centuries BC. The tragic hero collides with his destiny and his rebellion is condemned as madness. But that same rebellion is clothed in nostalgia for authentic freedom, a freedom that is not just a conscious submission to that faceless necessity before which even the gods tremble. Plato on occasion acknowledged doubt: was the "law and order of destiny," of the *einarmene*,[26] indeed identical to justice? Was that justice for which man thirsts in order to harmoniously regulate the city, that justice that would ensure that future Socrates would no longer be killed, was this indeed cosmic justice? Is evil only one necessary aspect of the whole order? Is it a degradation that is implicit in the apparent autonomy of the sensible world? Is it a form of non-being indispensable for the full deployment of being, a dissonance that is at the base of the whole symphony?

Books Six and Seven of *The Republic* go even further. If evil is born of the enslavement of the soul to a secret corruption, to a passion that reveals itself at the same time that it distorts discernment, then man cannot free himself without transcendent assistance, independent of his consciousness and his will. And the source of this liberation is not the world of ideas; it is that God who is beyond the intelligible, *"the beauty that is beyond all possibility of expression," "the good that surpasses being."* God alone can "save" man despite himself, in imposing exile and suffering on him through true grace (*theia moira*). This intuition of Plato's remains an isolated pointer. In the intellectual ambiance of the Hellenic epoch time became almost exclusively the symbol and locus of human enslavement, the mark of a tragic destiny bound

---

26. Plato, Laws, 904c.

by the stars to the opaque rotation of space. Instead of revealing eternity, time obscures it. Time as the realization of non-existence is opposed to eternity, a fullness that is ever more distant. This concludes in gnosis and gnosis yields an analysis of time that is almost identical to that of Buddhism.

The Manicheans had no difficulty in identifying the *metemsomatoses* to which men are condemned with the Buddhist wheel of *Sâmsâra*: men are trapped in the cycle and are transferred by death from one prison to another. This dismal repetition makes man a "stranger." He becomes separated from himself, from others, from being. Time breaks into scattered and fugitive moments that have no possible continuity. Time itself becomes a prison. The demonic lords, the *Archontes*, haunt the stars and keep the absurd mechanism of destiny in motion. The planets are alive with foul hallucinated life, hateful servants of the Demiurge, that mindless possessed laborer who blindly and in the darkness of isolation creates the fabric of the world, a cancerous tumor. The regularity of the stars is no longer a divine choir. It is a diabolical machine. Law ceases to be providence and becomes asphyxiation.

ΩΩΩ

"Where the Greeks exalted, accepted and consented, the Gnostics condemn, refuse and rebel."[27]

Time therefore becomes anguish and anguish becomes the foundation of existence in time. Man finds himself buried in the accidental, the detritus, the absence of sense. He is conceived in blind obscenity and is born in spasms of horror and bloody viscosity: he is no more than a bag of excrement that death will render into anonymous carrion to again return into one condemned to live.[28] Time, a never-completed process of destruction that is

---

27. Quoted from H.C. Puech, *Le Manichéisme.*
28. Marcion cited from Tertullian, *Adv. Marcionem.*

agony rather than death, therefore becomes identified with hell. The heaven of the spheres becomes an opaque canopy over hell, a hard ceiling whose starry vents are guarded by merciless jailers.

For the Manicheans in particular the passage of time is identified with life in hell. A demoniac, or possessed person, is a being without depth, entirely reduced to his temporal superficiality and held captive by his immediate present. He lives in the instant, that is to say, in a state of perpetual reduction to nothing that is combined with a perpetual renewal, in a repetitive discontinuity that condemns him to a vertiginous emptiness. To escape the emptiness he restricts himself to the moment and seeks to intensify it, in the end abandoning himself to the self-devouring death-wish. This *enthymesis* of death, analogous to Freud's death instinct, although with greater metaphysical depth, is perhaps the final word on the hell of temporal existence.

But what in fact is this time? Rather than the mirror of the divine it is a demonic caricature of eternity. Like Timaeus's demiurge, the gnostic demiurge constructs the future as an imitation of eternity. But Timaeus's demiurge contemplates eternity: the gnostic demiurge knows only nostalgia for its mother, fallen Wisdom. As the "fruit of absence" the demiurge creates only a phantom, a multiplicity of evil. At the limit time is nothing but an illusion and a lie. To tear off this veil of illusion that covers true eternity is an act of deliverance that wakens man from the nightmare of temporality. The "pneumatics," those who have purified themselves and are destined to salvation, attain their primary nature through gnosis. Having become wholly divine, they return to their eternal nature and become an abyss of freedom far above good and evil, those two poles of the same illusion. As for archaic religion, this gnostic eternity is a beyond, a lost and hidden paradise of pure gold in the midst of worldly corruption, a spark of hidden divinity at the core of the human spirit.

So what if this spirit, the unique essence of the elect of which it is the original form, occasionally takes the form of a savior, in order to arouse them? This savior comes in order to save himself, to assemble his own. Each spiritual person who becomes aware becomes his own savior, or rather, saves the savior who has been crucified by universal existence. This is the well-known dialectic of savior-saved, which in India is elaborated into the remarkable doctrine of self and avatar.

On the one hand there is an impersonal eternity in which man believes that he will discover, by diving into the gulf of his own solitude, that he is god by nature. On the other hand there is the gnostic drama of the eons, which have been called fragments of time rendered in space and hypostatized. This tragic conveyor does not so much lead man to God as lead from God to God, that is to say, from man back to himself. The multiplicity of the eons underscores the transcendence of the divine and makes it immanent in the intellect. The eternity of the gnostics, apparently so divine, is shown finally to be strangely human.

Indian philosophy elaborated a doctrine of the cosmic cycles that is both majestic and terrifying. There is a massive symphony of eons succeeding and absorbing each other, dissipating and swallowing up, with everything, from the thousand-year eon to the simple succession of instants in time, subject to the implacable law of cyclical time: appearance-dissolution; dissolution-appearance. A *mahâyuga* or cosmic cycle (a grand era) is made up of four "ages" or *yuga*. These are analogous to the "ages of the world" of Greek mythology. The *yuga* become shorter and shorter in duration, due to the acceleration of time, which is also the acceleration of the fall. Time shrinks to nothing and by its very duration exacerbates the cosmic-human condition. The Pancarâtra school links the doctrine of the "fall of wisdom" to the theory of cycles. The four Hindu ages take their names from four throws of the die: *krita*, *tretâ*, *dvâpara*, and *kali*. These correspond to the 4, 3, 2, and 1 of the die, and they have the corresponding durations. The *krita* or *satya yuga* is the age of accomplishment, the age of reality.[29] This corresponds to the paradisaical period of the archaic religions.

With the two succeeding ages mankind draws further and further away from *dharma* (that is, the law conceived as cosmic order) and the world of objects becomes more and more opaque as the universe begins to conceal *dharma* rather than reveal it:

---

29. From the verb *kri*: to make, accomplish, and *sat*: to be.

the universe ceases to be a theophany that nourishes contemplation and becomes an illusion that arouses desire and envy. In the *kali yuga*, the age of darkness, the age of evil, cosmic opacity and human egotism reign supreme. According to the *Vishnu Purâna*, society then reaches the stage where only property confers status, where only wealth inspires virtue, where only passion unites a man and a woman, where the lie is the only source of success in life, where sexuality is the only form of joy, and where ritualism has become identified with true religion. Such is the age in which mankind has been immersed for many centuries.

It is important to note that Hindu thought does not conceive of a linear succession of cosmic cycles. The 4-3-2-1 sequence embodies the flowering of paradise that is then submerged into darkness, and gives way to a new flowering. Each new cycle is grander than what came before and each one is condemned to destruction. A human *mahâyuga* lasts 12,000 years, but the divine *mahâyuga*, made up of 360 human *mahâyuga*, extends to 4,320,000 years. One thousand divine *mahâyuga* constitute a *kalpa* (form) and the *kalpa* is equivalent to one year in the life of Brahma. The life of Brahma, thus calculated, lasts for 36,000 *kalpa*, or 31 billion human years. But Brahma is not eternal: he is only the face of the absolute becoming manifest. One Brahma slowly and inexorably succeeds another, as they give birth to succeeding universes.

The repetition of the 4-3-2-1 cycle culminates in complete dissolution, in the *pralaya* and *mahâpralaya* in which all human, cosmic, and divine forms are absorbed into the sleep of Vishnu, the divine ontological root of all being. "Who can count the number of universes, each with its own Brahma? Beyond the furthest vision, beyond any imaginable space, universes are born and vanish without end. These universes float lightly on the pure and eternally deep water of the body of Vishnu. From each pore of this body a universe arises for an instant and explodes. Do you presume to count the number of universes?"[30] At each beat of the great Vishnu's eyelids a Brahma is extinguished.

---

30. Cited from the *Brahmavaivaru Purâna* (Hindu source), H. Zimmer, *Myths and Symbols in the Art and Civilization of India*, Paris, 1951.

The actual numbers invoked here are of little importance. The fantastic and terrifying magnitudes are aimed above all at rousing man from the sleep of daily life and the false sense of security of utilitarian time. They are aimed at making man feel the vertigo of time. In this regard Buddhism, stripping traditional Indian thought of its mythological content, calls the cosmic cycles "incalculable." In the perspective of endless repetition, all reality is stripped from temporal existence. Personal history, the history of the human race, even divine history, are all accounted evanescent and illusory. The *avatars*, manifestations of the absolute as savior of the world, are revealed to be merely an insignificant nightmare. In the *Puran* story, the symbolic boar takes the goddess Earth in his arms as he saves her from the depths of the sea, saying "every time that I carry you thus ---"

Ontologically, temporal existence is thus reduced to non-existence. In the cosmic negation of classical India, time is construed to be the very fabric of the *mâyâ*, that ambiguous reality and irreducible irrational core that reveals the total unreality of the most personal experience and of each loved one by hurling them into the whirlpool of eons and transfiguration. A folk tale will explain this more clearly than any further elaboration:

> Narâda, the model of piety, has gained the favor of Vishnu by his fervent asceticism. Narâda demanded that Vishnu reveal the power of his *mâyâ*. Vishnu replied with an ambiguous smile, "Will you go over yonder to fetch me a little water?" "Certainly, Master," replied Narâda as he began to walk toward a distant village. Vishnu waited in the shade of a rock for his return.

> Narâda knocked at the first door he came to. A very beautiful young woman opened it and the saintly man experienced something that he had never seen, even in a dream: he was spellbound by her eyes, which resembled those of his divine friend and master. He stood transfixed, forgetting why he had come. The young woman welcomed him in a friendly and

straightforward way. Her voice was like a gold cord passed around the neck of the stranger.

He entered as if in a dream. The occupants of the house greeted him respectfully. He was received with honor, but not exactly as a stranger, more as an old and venerable acquaintance who has been away for a long time. After a while he asked the father of the house for permission to marry his daughter. This is what everyone in the house had been waiting for. He became a member of the household, sharing their burdens and joys.

Twelve years passed. He had three children and when his father-in-law died he became head of the family, watching the cattle and cultivating the fields. In the twelfth year the rainy season was especially violent. The rivers were swollen and a torrential flood came down from the mountain and flooded the village. During the night the straw houses and the cattle were washed away and everyone fled. Holding his wife with one hand and guiding two of his children with the other, with the third child perched on his shoulders, Narâda left in great haste. He staggered along in the water, battered by the rain. Suddenly he stumbled. The child fell from his shoulders and disappeared into the roar of the night. Uttering a cry of despair, Narâda let go of the other children in order to grab the littlest one but he was too late. At this moment the raging water swept the other two children and his wife from his side.

He lost his own footing and was thrown into the torrent and landed, unconscious, on a rock. When he regained consciousness he could see only a vast expanse of muddy water and he wept for his loss. He heard a familiar voice, "My child, where is the water that you went to fetch for me? I have been waiting for almost half an hour." Narâda turned and saw the desert, scorched under the midday sun. Beside him Vishnu smiled with cruel tenderness: "Do you now understand the secret of my *mâyâ*?"[31]

For post-Vedic India, time is identified with the endurance of existence in a world of ignorance and pain. Ignorance—that is to say, attachment to desire and to the results of action—fuels the cycle of life and death and nails man to the wheel of a never-ending death. This "vertigo of time," this "dread of time," finds its final formulation in the "wheel of existence" of Buddhism. In the wheel of existence the present is continually transformed into the past, that is to say, into non-being. To use the language of existential philosophy, to which Buddhism is often very close, all existence in time is nothing other than a perpetual transformation into non-being. "The nature of each existing thing is its own instantaneity, created from an incalculable number of destructions of stasis."[32] And therefore "because the transformation into non-existence is instantaneous and uninterrupted, there is no movement."[33] Duration and the individual self, the "I," are no more than pragmatic constructs. Temporal existence, conceived as continual transformation into non-existence, signifies only the unreality of the universe.

In this context "deliverance" is the "flight from time" through illumination, transforming the illusory instant into the eternal present.

For ancient Greece, as for classical India, eternity is defined *in opposition* to time. Time is transformation into non-existence; eternity is the fulfillment of being. Time is mobile and transitory; eternity is stable and immobile. Both Buddhism and yoga make use of images of immobility to evoke the state of deliverance, as for example the immobile sun of the *Chândoya-Upanishad*. A

31. Folk tale as reported by Ramakrishna, *The Sayings of Sri Ramakrishna*, Madras, 1938.
32. Cantaraksita, *Tattvasangraha,* cited in M. Eliade, *Images and Symbols.*
33. Vasubandhu, *Abhidharmakoça,* cited in A. Coomaraswamy, *Time and Eternity,* 1947.

static eternity is thus opposed to time. All the dichotomous relationships that characterize temporal existence—self and other, the world (the mundane) and God (the sacred), time and eternity—are abolished in this static eternity.

The eternal state is not only the antithesis of dynamic time: in fact it swallows up dynamic time into the apophatic silence, the *neti-neti*, of the *Upanishads*, in which "this is not this, that is not that." There is nothing more that can be said of this all-absorbing eternity, because there is nothing else left. The ascetic path that leads to this absorption into eternity, or *entasis*, requires not repentance, *metanoia*, but the abolition of memory, including the subconscious and the collective subconscious. To accede to eternity is to transcend both time and self, by conquering memory, "congealed" time, a precipitate of the illusory postulate of the ego.

3.   Cyclical Time and Christianity

Before analyzing the ways in which the cyclical and biblical conceptions of time are opposed to each other, I would like to elucidate certain common features that enabled Christianity, as it
spread, to abolish the ancient laws through their fulfillment.

In my view, Christian and above all Orthodox spirituality
takes on board all the positive intuitions of cosmic religion. If the
reality of the Church is essentially eschatological, it is also a paradisaical reality, a paradise regained.[34] The saints live in harmony
with the wild animals and the wild animals recognize the scent of
the saints, that of Adam before the Fall. The saints, their essence
oriented toward God, contemplate the *logoï* of matter and of the
created world, as did Adam when he was in Paradise. Thus, as for
archaic man, the world appears as a "divine game." Our life, says
St. Maximus the Confessor, is only one moment in a dance: "truly,
we deserve to be called a game of God."[35]

This cosmic dance is reflected in the rhythm of the liturgy.
There are aspects of Orthodox spirituality that echo and appeal
to archaic nostalgia: existence viewed as a liturgical act, the solemnity of worship, sacred dance, and the "Holy, Holy, Holy" of
the liturgy; summing up, through the Christian lens, the whole
weight of contemplation and the blessing of nature. In the personal revelation of the Trinity, the presence of the Word and the
Spirit as Persons, the Church takes on what we may properly call
archaic spirituality, that is to say, the revelation of divine energy and the presence of the Word and the Spirit in the liturgy of
cyclical time. However, in integrating archaic religion, Christianity both exorcises and surpasses it. The dance of the liturgy

---

34. *"plantata est enim Ecclesia paradisus in hoc mundo."* St. Irenaeus, *Against
     the Heresies*, PG 7.
35. *De Ambigua*, PG 91 col 1416c. Translator's note: The "divine game" (lu-
     dus Dei) is quoted, in Maximus' original text, from Gregory Nazaianzus.
     Maximus comments that our present life, compared with our future divine
     life, is but a game. Our present life is flux and change, as compared to the
     stability of the heavens.

does not seek the dissolution of time into a static eternity that is at once pre-existent and co-existent. Instead, the liturgy of the Church unveils and celebrates the true eternity that, rather than being opposed to time, is revealed in the very heart of temporal existence. Paradise regained is already surpassed in the Second Coming (the Parousia). The liturgical "participation in universal existence" culminates in the personal encounter.

High culture systematizations, particularly those of post-Vedic India, are much further from Christianity than the intuitions of archaic religion. In them, the I-thou relationship between man and God that is so widely found in archaic religions is displaced by an impersonal conception of the Absolute, conceived of not as "thou" but as "that." At the same time nostalgia for the time of paradise, for the archaic encounter of time and eternity, gives way to the search for fusion in an undifferentiated unity of time and eternity, in which time is merely the illusory aspect of eternity.

Nevertheless, the Hindu "dread of time" finds its echo in Orthodox ascetic practice, insofar as the latter attempts to abolish and escape fallen temporal existence, the time of sin and death, without, however, seeking to abolish time itself. For the Orthodox ascetic, the world of fallen humanity and of ordinary human temporal existence is vain and illusory. For St. John the Theologian and for St. Paul, being according to the world or according to the flesh is being according to death, *eis thanaton*. For the end of all things is death. If you live according to the flesh you will die.[36] In the New Testament texts sadness over the state of the world and despair over existence according to the flesh has echoes of both the Buddhist analysis of time and of Heidegger's *geworfenheit*.[37]

Must we therefore suppose a Buddhist influence on the doctrine of cosmic illusion that we find in Origen and St. Gregory of Nyssa? Would it not suffice for them to have meditated upon the Bible, which itself comments at length on the destructive cycle of

---

36. Romans 6:21
37. Translator's note: *geworfenheit*: the state of having been thrown into the world.

temporal existence? *"Vanity, vanity, saith the Preacher, all is vanity."*[38] In the Fathers we again find the vertiginous whirlpool of cosmic time, the endless cycle of life and death that characterizes Indian thought. We find almost the same symbols being used: the spider's web, as when St. Gregory of Nyssa describes terrestrial existence as a web of illusion woven from futile cares; the dream-mirage, which arouses deceptive images of grandeur, wealth, and pleasure in the intellect, images of everything sought by frivolous people, all to vanish with the passage of ephemeral time; and finally, enchantment, the varied illusion of temporal life which has captured mankind as though it had drunk Circe's magic potion and had been led to abandon its true nature in favor of an immoral existence.[39]

St. Isaac says, "the world is a lady of ill-repute drawing toward her all those who contemplate her, desirous of her beauty."[40] The sorceress Circe, a lady of ill-repute—these images are so close to the cosmic enchantment denoted by *mâya*. For the Fathers, this cosmic enchantment is that of cyclical time, in which desire is perpetually reborn to be once again thwarted in an endless stasis, the image of pure multiplicity. "It is a children's game played in the sand," says Gregory of Nyssa, "a sand hill that collapses as fast as it is built." In this way, the Orthodox ascetic's "memory of death" is similar to the Hindu "dread of time." The difference is that creation itself, and this includes creation's temporal dimension, is not and cannot be placed into question. Indian thought by contrast does not know of the "creation," only of the "manifestation," of matter. What the Orthodox ascetic challenges is not the created being, but non-being, that constitutes a parasitic precipitate formed from the fundamental freedoms of the created being. For India, the spider's web is the cosmos itself, woven by the Absolute. For Gregory of Nyssa, the spider's web is merely a mesh of illusion cast over the goodness of creation by the "Prince of Deception." The Hindu ascetic works to become aware that he is nothing: the Christian ascetic works to become aware that he is unworthy and of no repute.

---

38. Ecclesiastes 1:4-9
39. St. Gregory of Nyssa, *Commentary on Ecclesiastes*.
40. St. Isaac the Syrian, Sentence 37.

The Hindu ascetic wishes to abolish time by destroying memory: the Christian ascetic purifies time through repentance.

Although we have noted the ways in which the religious thought of classical India marks a retreat from the intuitions of archaic religion, we should nevertheless note that, since the beginning of the Christian era, the Hindu and Buddhist East has increasingly sought out a personal god and has thus begun to conceive of time as the locus for that possible encounter. The theological import of this cannot be over-emphasized. In India, as in medieval China, mystical love, the adoration of the transcendent Lord, took an increasingly important place at the expense of gnosis, the search for arcane knowledge. The everyday religion of contemporary India is completely steeped in the "way of love," *bhakti*, and in Tantrism. The grand master of *bhakti*, Râmânuja, the heir to the great Tamil mystical poets who sang of the nuptial embrace of the soul and the Lord, would not accept the unfolding present as a sacrificial process in which love itself is destroyed, in the dissolving of the one who loves into the one who is loved. For Râmânuja, man and God are neither completely distinct nor completely merged: they are united as "the body is to the soul." The unfolding present is thus filled with the radiance of God and becomes the body of eternity, permitting the loving encounter of man and God. One can describe Tantrism as an irresistible resurgence of archaic intuitions. In time and in the universe, the Tantric practitioner discovers the means to participate in divine energy and in God's universal presence, in his cosmic game. Through time, he is able embrace the *mâya*, which is henceforth understood not as illusory enchantment but as *shakti*, divine energy. "The perfect practitioner is able to see into the depths and to grasp the loving embrace of life and the universe as the revelation of supreme divine energy. The omnipresent Divine being is experienced in his cosmic play of freedom."[41]

In the Far East, Buddhism, oriented in its origins to the inner potential of man, has become a religion of compassion and faith. Its central focus is no longer the Buddha, the enlightened

---

41. H. Zimmer, *Les Philosophies de l'Inde*, Paris, 1953.

one, but the Bodhisattva, who turns away from solitary contemplation to assist all men, and indeed all sentient beings, in their
passage through time. At the moment that Avalôkitesvara, the
great Mayanistic Bodhisattva, was about to enter into the supreme
peace of Nirvana, all creation cried out in lamentation, seeing itself abandoned to temporal existence. And so the Bodhisattva re-
nounced pursuit of the fullness of Nirvana until all beings, without
exception, should be ready to enter with him, "just as the Good
Shepherd first lets his flock pass through and then enters himself
before closing the door." Here, at the limit of time and eternity
the Bodhisattva realizes his vow: "I wanted to be a guardian for
those who are without protection, a guide for the voyager, a boat, a
well, a spring, a bridge for those who seek the further bank."[42] Thus
time, experienced in *bhakti* as the place of encounter between man
and God, and in Tantrism as a cosmic sacrament, is experienced
in compassionate Buddhism as mediation and grace.

However, this orientation to time is tentative and is always
threatened by the concept of an undifferentiated unity, by the
vast whirlpool of eternity. Râmânuja does not know of the fundamental doctrines of creation and the Trinity and conceives of
the creature as an emanation of the creator. Tantrism identifies
divine energy with the cosmos itself. Buddhism denies the reality
of the created world as it seeks to resolve the contradiction between endless cyclical repetition and the expectation of the final
entry of all beings into Nirvana. "All beings must be led by me
into Nirvana," says the Bodhisattva in the Diamond Sutra. But
not one single being has yet entered Nirvana. And why is this? If
a Bodhisattva should perceive being as reality then he cannot be
called illumined. And so the non-Christian East has not yet discovered the full meaning of time. But the existential orientation
of these doctrines prepares the ground for the personal time of
the Bible, for the time of encounter. The poet Râmprasâd perhaps
states this best in an image. He is reported to have said, "I love to
eat sugar but I do not wish to become sugar."[43]

---

42. L. de La Vallée Poussin, *Bouddhisme*, Paris, 1925.
43. Cited from *The Gospel of Sri RamaKrishna,*, New York, 1942.

Part Two

God and Time

"The following question deserves sustained inquiry; how can that which is always present come into the world?"[44]

---

44. St. Gregory of Nyssa, *De Pauperibus Amandis*, PG 46.

1.   The New Structures of Time

Before proceeding to study the linear time of the Old Testament
and the transfigured time of the New Testament, I would like to
point out certain temporal structures, found both in the Scriptures
and in the Fathers, that make clear the completely new and henceforth fundamental value that the Judeo-Christian revelation confers on time, history, and personal revelation. There are four major inter-related propositions that express this reappraisal of time:

I   The eternal nature of the Living God cannot be
        defined as an exception to time.

II   Time, speaking metaphorically, is a creature and
        therefore, as is true of all creation, it is good and
        has meaning.

III   The value of time is inextricably linked to the
        revelation of personhood and love.

IV   In the Parousia, in the Kingdom, time does not so
        much disappear as become transfigured.

I.   The eternal nature of the Living God cannot be
     defined as an exception to time.

When the Bible depicts God acting in the world, it makes use of
the categories of everyday life, love, anger, and even repentance.
This anthropomorphism, rooted as it is in everyday life, is much
less cumbersome than that of the metaphysicists, whose categories always refer to space and matter. The categories of the Bible
are those of life itself, based in time and the individual, based in
time as the realization of personhood. This does not, however,
mean that the eternity of the Living God is simply an indefinite
duration, that of a consciousness with a past without beginning
and a future without end. When Oscar Cullmann wrote that
"time, in its indefinite duration, begins with God," that is to say

that time is without beginning, he stumbled into contradicting both the Bible and himself. In his chapter on "The sovereignty of God over time" he wrote "God is above time and rules over time."[45] These simple words "above" and "over" convey, in accordance with all of Scripture, that which we call eternity, which is nothing other than the presence of that God who is beyond and above time. "We confess you, Lord of time and of the present. Everything passes but you remain eternally the same."[46] When St. John writes "in the beginning was the word and the word was with God and the word was God," it is very clear that he is speaking of an eternal beginning and of God's life itself, of the eternal present of the Trinity. Time, as Cullmann showed, is the product of divine "economy." But divine "economy" has no other purpose than to reveal the Lord of the world himself, in his living intimacy and his living eternity, as "the mystery hidden from all time and in all ages,"[47] or more precisely hidden *for* all time and all ages, but now made manifest.

On the day of his manifestation, Christ himself said no more than "I am" in order to convey his Godhood. This "I am" is placed beyond daily life in eternity. *"Truly, truly I say unto you, before Abraham was, I am."*[48] The present tense affirms a reality that is not antecedent to a given moment in time but that transcends time itself. This is the irreducibly eternal present of "theology"—where "theology" is the divine reality in and of itself as opposed to "economy" through which "theology" is revealed to the world.

The symmetry of a "before" and an "after" placed in unlimited time with respect to the present eon does not present a proper conception of time.

It is instead a weak spatial schematic of the sort that Bergson freed us from, and that contrary to the images of the Bible, devalues history, rather than giving it weight and value. In this

---

45. Cullmann, p. 34.
46. Syrian Liturgy, Evening Office.
47. Colossians 1:28
48. John 8:58 (RSV)

infinite expanse of time, the present becomes an insignificant instant. We have escaped from the engulfing static eternity of the non-Christian East only to fall into the sterile infinity of a mathematical series. Biblical anthropomorphism, on the other hand, demonstrates that eternity is oriented toward time and that eternity sustains and marches with time toward encounter and fulfillment. Biblical anthropomorphism confirms the positive value of time, in which the dialogue between God and man matures and in which the wedding feast of the Creator and the created is prepared and celebrated. In the biblical perspective, time is neither opposed to eternity nor is eternity reduced to time. The relationship between time and eternity is better conceived of in terms of courtship and nuptial encounter, extending from the interrupted courtship in Paradise to the "let it be according to thy word" of Mary; from the mystery of the God-man-hood of Christ to the mystery of the Church as the incarnation of the Kingdom on earth; from the wedding at Cana to the final banquet in the Kingdom. In fact the Fathers, true to the historical focus of the Bible, avoided defining the eternity of the divine through opposition to time, which is dynamic, based on movement and change. The Fathers do not oppose an unchanging eternity pregnant with being[49] to an illusory future, in which change is equivalent to degradation and evil. Orthodox theology avoids defining God as unchangeable, immutable, and invariable, and in this respect is much less burdened by the Platonic concepts that Western theology, following St. Augustine, introduced into the very conception of God.

Of course, theologians are acquainted with that immobile eternity at which both Platonism and Indian thought halt, which is static with regard to rational thought and "enstatic" with regard to mystical experience. In contemplation, the "gnosis of reality," *ta onta*, corresponds to the Platonic *cosmos noetos,* which St. Maximus the Confessor calls the "eternity of eons." Proportion, truth, the unchangeable structures of the cosmos, the geometry that orders creation, the symphony of mathematical rhythm, are

---

49. In Greek philosophy the unchangeable is equal to the Good.

all stable and immutable and they confer coherence and intelligibility on the perceived universe. Time and eon are facets of one another: the eon is immobile time, and time is the eon measured out in movement.[50] The world of visible things is, in fact, immobile in its nature, in its order, and in its persistence. One substance never leaves its natural domain to change into another or to become admixed. And yet the material world is a perpetual flux and reflux. When, in contemplation, "the world of sense perception is perceived as entirely and gnostically immanent to the whole intelligible world,"[51] the universe ceases to be exterior to the contemplative. "The purified heart becomes an inner heaven with its own sun, its moon and its stars."[52] However, this state of complete interiorization, in which the intellect rejoins its "true state," is not knowledge of true eternity. Evagrius's abstract teaching on the gnosis of the absolute, *gnosis ousiodes,* which is very close to the Hindu teaching on the "escape from time," was both absorbed and surpassed by the great ascetic Orthodox teachings. In the Philokalia one anonymous father says, "the *noûs* will be perfect when it has completely brought down the *gnosis ousiodes*." The eternity of the eons is not in fact divine eternity. Paradoxically, the eternity of the eons is part of creation. Lossky writes, "the intelligible is not eternal: it has its beginning in secular time, in the eons, in the passage from non-being into being."[53]

For St. Maximus, the world is "the closed house" in which time is reflected in the eon and the eon in time, whose perfect center lies in the "ex-centric" transcendence of God.[54] "God is

---

50. St. Maximus the Confessor, *De Ambigua*, PG 91.
51. St. Maximus the Confessor, *Mystagogia*, PG 91.
52. Philothea of Syria, *On Sobriety*.
53. V. Lossky, op. cit. 97-98.
54. Hans Urs von Balthasar, Cosmic Liturgy, Ignatius Press, San Francisco, 2003. Translator's note: The "closed house" is a concept that Clément takes directly from von Balthasar. "In its radical openness to the transcendent, the world is thus indeed the "closed house" that Aristotle and Gregory of Nyssa had conceived it to be, a whole 'that needs no addition and no subtraction, in order to become better'" (op. cit. p.151) . . . "The unity that is fulfillment, the real heart of the world, can thus only be transcendent, far from the mainstream of ordinary life (ex-zentrisch) . . . God's tran-

above all beings, those that circumscribe and those that are cir-cumscribed, because He is beyond any interdependence." Divine eternity transcends both the constant change characteristic of time and the immutability characteristic of the eon. "God is not changed in any way: nor is He stillness, as this can only be as-cribed to a circumscribed being whose nature has a beginning."[55] Apophatic silence bars us from envisioning the Living God ac-cording to the cold eternal progression of mathematical laws. The biblical revelation of a personal God shows him wholly engaged in history. Ultimately, the Incarnation reveals the fullness of the Trinity, clothed in the humble cloth of temporal existence, in the historical existence of Christ.

"And the word became flesh and dwelt among us . . . No one has seen God: only the Son, who is in the bosom of the Father, who has made him known."[56] The Living God contains all that is positive of temporal existence. He both reconciles and surpass-es stasis and kinesis. On the cross, the Eternal-become-Tempo-ral draws into himself all that is negative in temporal existence. This act not only annihilates all that is negative but also inverts its meaning, saturating the negative with light, so that henceforth "the glory as of the only Son from the Father"[57] is conveyed in time through all aspects of temporal existence. Thus time is re-

---

scendence is the ultimate basis for the possibility of a balance and imaging of intellect and matter. The world becomes, once again, a 'closed house;' it is God's mirror, in that it ceaselessly realizes, in the heart of its reality, the uncanny reciprocal reflectivity of intellect and matter" (op. cit. p. 176). Von Balthasar and, by extension, Clément appear to borrow the term "the closed house" from the last of Paul Claudel's Cinq Grandes Odes, La Mai-son Fermée. In this long prose poem, "the closed house" represents, first, the poet, who has turned himself ascetically away from the world; then the closed sanctuary in which he discovered God; then the sanctified state of marriage, in which a person steps ascetically out of the bounds of himself into a greater belonging, that is rooted in love, for one's spouse, for one's child, for mankind; and finally "the closed house" represents the open-ing up to the mystery and vastness of the divine. See Paul Claudel, *Cinq Grandes Odes*, N.R.F. Paris, 1913, reissued in Gallimard, Collection Poésie, 1966.

55. Maximus the Confessor, De Ambigua, PG 91.
56. John 1:14, 18 (RSV)
57. John 1:14 (RSV)

vealed not as opposition to eternity but as the vessel chosen by God to receive and communicate the truth of eternity. In this regard, Cullmann correctly notes that the atemporality of the Platonic conception of eternity is completely inconsistent with the history of salvation. True eternity cannot be the negation of temporal existence, since through time the Eternal chose to reveal himself. Man cannot open himself to the eternity of God by turning his back on temporal existence. The encounter with the eternal ripens in time, through the lived moments of hope, faith, and love. These moments are both fully in time and fully eternal, just as Christ is both wholly God and wholly man.

Perhaps, to sum up, we can evoke this mysterious eternity of the Living God by looking at the multiple meanings of the word "present." The three divine hypostases are completely *present* to one another and in this way *present* divine nature in its fullness, in the eternity of life and love in which they dwell, in the eternal *present* that transcends both the mutable and the immutable. In contrast to the ideal world of Plato, this eternal present is not accessible in time to the contemplative intellect, as it is contained wholly within a personal presence, for whom the world of ideas is an instrument of his sovereign will. And this sovereign intent is to give eternity to man as a gift, as grace, as personal encounter that culminates in the "we shall see face to face." "And this is the life everlasting, that they know You, the only true God and Jesus Christ, Whom You sent."[58]

For one person to give himself to another, he must be received. Thus contained within a personal God, eternity is inserted into history as the most beautiful gift of love. The one who in the radiance of his nature is always present had to patiently follow the path of history in order to be welcomed as man. "The following question deserves sustained inquiry; how can that which is always present come into the world?"[59] The presentness of the divine energies becomes waiting and expectation. Such is the mystery of the "acceptable time" of the *kairos* prepared by the Lord

---

58. John 17:3
59. St. Gregory of Nyssa, *De Pauperibus Amandis*, PG 46.

and enacted by the Son and the Holy Spirit, the mystery of those moments when he who is always present comes to meet mankind.

II.   Time, speaking metaphorically, is a creature and therefore, as is true of all creation, it is good and has meaning.

According to the biblical revelation, the world is not eternal, nor was it created at a certain moment out of the flux of eternity, out of time without end. If this were the case then time could be again destroyed and recreated. The Bible reveals time and the world created together at the same moment, in a single act. We therefore cannot objectify the original void or place it in time. "Void" means that before the creation nothing existed except God and nothing existed outside of God. In fact the concepts of "before" and "outside of" are absurd, as they only have meaning in the framework of the creation. The act of creation gives birth to time, the signifiers of which are "before" and "after." The concepts "before God" and "outside of God" lead only to the limits of thought where thought is abolished. In order to explain the "beginning" of which Genesis speaks, the Fathers, St. Gregory of Nyssa and St. Basil in particular, employ Plato's profound insight on the "sudden."[60] This strange form of reality is situated between movement and rest. It is not in time. It is the point of arrival and the point of departure for the mutable, which changes into its resting state, and the immutable, which changes into movement. This experience of the instant, which anyone can have at certain privileged moments of their existence, is in essence none other than an intuition of the creative influx flowing from the source of one's being. It is a participation in the very moment of creation, in the first irruption of the "sudden." This is where the truth of archaic religions is to be found, insofar as they exalt that moment of revelation, not as an escape into an always accessible parallel eternal world, but as a renewal of the moment of paradise, as a

60. Plato, *Parmenides*, 157.

descent toward the original and always life-giving influx of life. In this regard, St. Gregory of Nyssa plays with the words *genesis*, becoming, and *gennesis*, perpetual birth.[61]

The Fathers made legitimate use of Plato's intuition on the nature of the "sudden." For the Fathers, the "in the beginning" of Genesis is a "sudden" event at the limit (in the strict mathematical sense) of eternity and time. As St. Basil so well demonstrated, it is an instant that is out of time itself but whose creative force gives birth to time. One might say that this instant is the point of contact between the divine will and that which at that moment begins, and does not cease to begin, passing from non-being into being, which becomes and endures. Because of the exact and timeless moment of creation it was said, "In the beginning, God created," as the beginning is something unseen and without dimension. Just as the beginning of a path is not yet the path and as the foundation stone of a building is not yet the building, so the beginning of time is not yet time itself. It is not even the very smallest instant of time. If one claims that the beginning occurs in time then this beginning must necessarily be divided into the categories of time, with a beginning, a middle, and an end. It is absurd to imagine the beginning of the beginning. And once one begins one cannot stop: each beginning divides itself into a further beginning and so on, ad infinitum. By stating "In the beginning, God created," Genesis instructs us how the world was brought into existence in time by the timeless divine will.[62]

In a footnote to *Christ and Time*, Cullmann gives an answer to those who wish to know what God did in his time of rest before the creation, the answer that Augustine has used before him: "God was not idle—he created hell for those who ask too many questions." Calvin also refused to answer this question, saying that God went out into the forest to collect switches for those who ask useless questions. Like St. Augustine before them, the Protestant reformers understood the creation from nothing, ex nihilo, as an event at the limit and showed by the use of humor how thought

61. St. Gregory of Nyssa, *De Vita Moysis*.
62. St. Basil, *Homilies on the Hexameron*, SC 26.

itself is ineluctably abolished when it tries to leap outside of time. It is therefore regrettable that Cullmann speaks of "facts prior to the beginning," without realizing that in so doing he strips away meaning from the words "creation" and "beginning."[63] If time is not part of creation, it is uncreated and if so, it is God: in which case, how could God have mastery over time?

Gregory of Nyssa understood that the cosmos is intrinsically temporal and that one cannot separate created nature and the unfolding present. In perpetual transition from non-being into being, the created is embedded in change and temporality. "The eon is the limit of mankind's movement and spiritual activity."[64] Time provides the necessary space and distance for man to be other than God, without however becoming fully self-sufficient. For St. Gregory of Nyssa, *diastema* or *diastasis*—distancing—are synonymous with the eon, at once finite in time and with infinite potential for a fullness that is wholly other. For St. Gregory, creation is always a distancing and therefore is ontologically in time.

Thus time is the very fabric of creation, or rather, to avoid a spatial metaphor, it is the rhythm and fundamental polarity of creation. Time is the most intimate dimension of the person, as we shall later see clearly. One can even propose, with allowance given for poetic approximation, that time is a creature and that as such it is completely good. It is time that gives its pulse to the divine benedictions of Genesis: "and he saw that it was good." To the extent that we are far removed from awareness of deified time, as revealed by the Church, it is difficult for us to imagine the splendor of time for the early Church, the Church of Paradise.

As fallen beings our awareness of time is irrevocably tied to death, and to some extent knowledge of time is a "*memento mori.*" Likewise, it is hard for us to conceive of *eros*, the love experienced in Paradise, as for us the succession of generations is necessarily linked to mortality and corruption. In the time of Paradise, God was present to man and conversed with him. Day succeeded day in a majestic diurnal rhythm that gave birth to new beginnings

---

63. Cullmann, *Christ and Time.*
64. St. Gregory of Nyssa, *Contra Eunomymium*, PG 45.

without rupture, to a propitious diversity, a multiplicity of being made for the expansion of love, in a duration made for a nature striving toward God. Time was thus a kind of permanent miracle, in the sense that the miracle restores nature to its original dynamism, and frees it from the laws by which it had been paralyzed through the Fall. This was the time of a festive world to which we are restored, however fleetingly, in certain moments of friendship and certain artistic experiences. Saint Exupéry called these the Feast of the Encounter.[65] Indeed, this was the time of friendship and espousal: man and God walked together in the cosmic garden, entranced by each other, talking together in the cool air of the evening, in the breath of the spirit. This was a time of Paradise without the dull repetition and sadness of the "end time." It was the time of a perpetual "for the first time."

But time was profoundly corrupted by the Fall, which inextricably admixed time and death. Time was given to man on the basis of his insufficiency so that as he moved from insufficiency to fulfillment it would become a movement of love, a dynamic of adoration. Instead, in his claim to be self-sufficient in his state of insufficiency, man transformed time into pure non-identity, reducing it to non-being. The time of miracles became the time of endless repetition. The time of Paradise became the time of absence. The time of opening to fullness became the time of condensation into vanity and non-being.[66] The paradisaical time of ascent is now the time of Satan's fall. It is no longer the passage from non-being into being. It is instead a passage from being into a vertiginous, insatiable, and ever more ferocious drive toward annihilation.[67] This is time made up of many dead instants, of lost time, of never again. It is time that uses up and mechanizes existence, time that opens onto the uncertain certitude of death, time that sin—that is, separation from one's neighbor and from God—has endowed with the opacity of death. The most lucid experience it as anxiety; the rest experience it as a flight into daily

65. A. de Saint Exupéry, *Lettre à un Otage*, p. 34.
66. Romans 8:20
67. Genesis 3:17-18

cares and diversions. On occasion, faced with the voice of the serpent of old, who asks the terrible and irrevocable question, "What
good will come of all of this?" we answer with an irresistible urge
to suicide. Fallen time in its fallen state must destroy itself. "And
God saw that the evil of man on earth was so great and that his
heart's desire was only to form evil plans all day long, and God
repented of having made man for the earth"[68] and God allowed
the world to slide and begin to dissolve itself into the waters of the
second day of creation.

But time is not entirely fallen. Time is not completely identified with the Fall, because the "vanity" of which St. Paul speaks
is not, in contrast to the Hindu *mâyâ,* time itself, but its vampire.
It was the man Noah who testified that time could "march with
God," even if it no longer carried the assurance of the ascension of
the created toward the uncreated. Noah demonstrated that time,
even in its opacity, could become the medium of the promise of
faithfulness and of alliance. With Noah, time received stability
and grace from God: "as long as the earth endures, summer and
winter, day and night, will never end."[69] From that moment, time
has become God's vehicle, witnessing to his wisdom through
its rhythms. God introduced duration—of blood-ties, sex, and
death—into his creation of love and into what we may call his
pedagogy. As St. Irenaeus explained, God drew man away from
the tree of life not through vengeance but through love. Having
turned away from God, man was in a state of spiritual death and
could not become part of eternity. If he had entered eternity in
that state of death, he would have suffered the torments of hell.
There is sweet sadness in physical death, which brings to an end
the spiritual death that is separation from God. According to St.
Irenaeus, "God put death as a limit to man's transgression. With
death sin ceases. A term is assigned to man by his return to the
dust so that one day he will cease to live in sin, so that he will die
to sin and begin to live in God."[70]

---

68. Genesis 6:5-6
69. Genesis 8:22
70. St. Irenaeus, Against the Heresies.

The divine pedagogue uses the momentum of the Fall, which continues and even accelerates through the course of human history. Progress, according to St. Irenaeus, is the long journey to awareness of the true condition of man, through the many revolts and turnings away from God. Time brings to naught man's claims to autonomy. Death causes pride to crumble. This is so that, at the end of the night, man will choose to obey and adore, in full knowledge, and will transform the immense emptiness of his misery into the container of grace.

When the completely lucid experience of fallen time leads man back to the experience of having been cast out, leaving no other options than death or absolution, then the Son can descend to death and be reborn. Then man will "know by experience from what evil he has been delivered."[71] "God allowed man to be swallowed by the leviathan, not in order to see him disappear and perish completely, but because he had established and prepared in advance the salvation accomplished by the Word, according to the 'sign' of Jonah: I called to the Lord, out of my distress, and he answered me; out of the belly of Sheol I cried and thou didst hear my voice."[72] Fallen time is confirmed for Noah and his sons by God's benediction. It is a necessary ordeal: the Fathers insist at length on the necessity of *peira*,[73] thanks to which the soul, satiated with sin, can freely turn toward God and understand the immensity of his love.[74]

III.   The value of time is inextricably linked to the revelation of personhood and love.

The time of trial, succeeding the time of espousal, embeds the true value of temporal existence in the person and in love. The Creator indeed risked something new as "poet of heaven and earth." He fulfilled his all-powerfulness by accepting the creation

---

71. St. Irenaeus, Against the Heresies.
72. St. Irenaeus, Against the Heresies.
73. Translator's note: *peira* means experience or trial.
74. Origen, *De Principiis*.

of another free being, as the ultimate challenge. By free love, God
decides to enter into a reciprocal relationship with his creature.
He would create other gods, but cannot do so without their consent. God wishes to adopt man, but he cannot insist. And so his
omnipotence is curiously bounded in its fulfillment. The mas-
terpiece of creation, the calling forth of another being, implies
the absolute *kenosis* of the Creator. It demands the humility, the
discretion, the patient waiting of the one who loves first without receiving, who cannot enforce love. God wants to give himself entirely and knows that he will go so far as to give himself
to man even in the abyss of the hell of man's hatred and refusal.
For this reason the Apocalypse and St. Paul speak of the lamb
slaughtered from the foundation of the world.[75] Creation cannot
set itself up against God: it exists only through and by virtue of his
free will. St. Philaret of Moscow said, "created beings are placed
on the creative word of God as on a diamond bridge that passes
beneath the infinitude of the divine and above the abyss of their
own non-being."[76] "When thou takest away their breath they die
and are turned again to their dust,"[77] sings the Psalmist. But it is
God's will that man should be free, it is his creative grace. That is
why God allows himself to be ignored and refused. It is why man
can turn away from his Creator and organize the world as his own
kingdom without being destroyed, even to the point, so to speak,
of casting God out of his own creation. God can multiply pun-
ishments and miracles but the love that he awaits from man cannot be merely the terrorized submission of a slave or an animal's
hypnotic attraction. Man as person must give himself freely. The
creation opens the door on a history that does not know of a *deus
ex machina*, only of the time of preparation and communion.

Time is therefore both a test of human freedom and, mov-
ingly, of God's expectation. As Martin Buber noted, the biblical
metaphysics of time are also those of dialogue, of an authentic dialogue in which the word of man has as much weight as the word

---

75. Revelation 13:8
76. Cited by Lossky.
77. Psalm 104:29 (BCP)

of God. God awaits the human word. He wants to be interrupted. "I heard the voice of the Eternal saying whom shall I send and who will go for us, and Isaiah offered himself saying send me."[78] In certain places the Bible "naively" reveals God's desire to share his disquietude. Should he hide from Abraham what he is about to do? God does not act without revealing his secrets to his servants and to his prophets. It is not just God's gift to man to reveal himself; it is also an appeal to man. The "where are you" expresses the sadness of God confronted with Adam, who has turned away from him. The *Midrash Tanhuma* says that sin inflicts less harm on man than on God, a Jewish interpretation that is profoundly Christian in how it shows the *kenosis* of God's divinity, both in the time of freedom to which he gives birth and in the time of sin that he accepts. This is the sacrificial patience that allows the being of the fallen world to stand before the face of him who is the Truth, the Judge, and the All-Powerful.[79] And so we come to understand that the mystery of divine eternity could not be revealed except through the *kenosis* of the Son, that is to say, in time.

In unveiling the freedom of God and man, the Bible inverts the relationship that primitive religion and antiquity established between space and time, between the cosmos and history. Time, for the Greeks above all, is absorbed back into space through the mediation of the stars, to take its place in the closed fullness of the cosmos. To reach the divine, man depersonalizes himself, joining himself to the cosmos and to the "procession of the stars which forms the choir for the most beautiful and magnificent dance, fulfilling that which ought to be for all living beings."[80] By contrast, space in the Bible is ordered by time, by the encounter between man and God. History, as the mystery of grace and freedom, replaces the cosmos as the measure of balance and perfection. Henceforth freedom makes equilibrium impossible to achieve. Nietzsche was not mistaken in reproaching Christianity for having destroyed the self-contained beauty of the classical

---

78. Isaiah 6:8
79. S. Bulgakov, *The Paraclete*, p. 369.
80. Plato, *Epinomis*.

universe. The cosmos is no longer the end of all things, bound in cyclical immobility. Instead the end is the union of God and man and universal transfiguration. Until this union is realized, thus exploding history, restless disquiet will roam the world and any search for equilibrium, for so-called total order, will be only demonic temptation and flight from God.

The dimension of freedom, the space-coordinate in the time of the encounter, is already declared in the Old Testament: "you will no longer be called Jacob but Israel, because you have wrestled with God."[81] The chosen people, chosen for such a demanding obedience, are precisely those who are the most untamed, the most recalcitrant. Jacob wrestles with the angel, Isaiah and Jeremiah rebel, Jonah flees. But in the end they accomplish what God has demanded of them. Subjection is replaced by the dialectic of personal engagement, in which to be a person is to be free. Christ reveals the meaning of this freedom when he gives his disciples power over demons, more power even than Adam had before the Fall. Christ says, "do not rejoice in this, that the spirits submit to you, but rejoice because your names are written in Heaven."[82] The name designates the person, and the personal destiny of the Christian is thus placed in the heaven of the divine presence, beyond the stars and the planets.

Plato thought the regularity of the stars' path proved their divinity, because "they always act in the same way, their deliberations do not change in any direction, sometimes deciding one thing and sometimes another, changing their orbit and going wandering."[83] The early Christian Lactance turned this argument on its head, witnessing to the new reign of freedom: "Precisely because the stars cannot leave their prescribed orbits it is apparent that they are not gods. If they were gods, we would see them going hither and thither like living beings on earth, who go where they will, because they have free will."[84] For St. Methodius

----

81. Genesis 32:29
82. Luke 10:20
83. Plato, *Epinomis*.
84. Institutions Divines

of Olympus, man in his freedom is superior to the heavens and to the sun, which slavishly carry out the will of God.

God created man in his own image, he calls him by name, and man acts in a free personal relationship with his Creator. Human destiny transcends that of the universe. In early Christianity, the "humiliation" of the stars rings out as a hymn of praise to grace and freedom. Man is not only greater than the cosmos: he alone can give it sense. The fate of the created universe depends on the history of salvation, as St. Paul shows.[85] The biblical revelation compels us to reject antiquity's conception of time, as well as the contemporary mathematical concept of time as the fourth dimension of the universe. If time is the fourth dimension, we are again trapped in the cosmos, albeit one situated in an expanding universe. Three dimensional space in its entirety is, as it were, the dimension and the matrix of the history of salvation, the highway of an unrepeatable journey, the highway along which man flees from the God who is seeking him, the highway of the pilgrimage of God to man, and then of man to God. On the vertical dimension, Christ is the highway to the Father, by which God comes to meet us in the horizontal dimension of history. The cross reveals history becoming the flesh of the Incarnation, the Church of the Holy Spirit.

IV.   In the Parousia, in the Kingdom, time does not so much disappear as become transfigured.

If time is summoned to reveal eternity, if time's entering into eternity constitutes the whole meaning of history, what will become of time when the fullness of the end is revealed, when God will be "all in all"? When the mystery of God is fulfilled, says the Apocalypse, "there shall be no more time."[86] The Apocalypse announces the abolition of night and the end of dependence on the light

---

85.   Romans chapter 8
86.   Revelation 10:6

of the sun[87] "for the glory of God illuminates it, and its lamp is
the lamb."[88] In fact, the Second Coming, like the primordial void,
constitutes a limiting concept for our reflection on time, as there
can be no "after."

But just as the best of temporal existence allows us to evoke
divine eternity not as cold immobility but as Love and Life, so
we can postulate that positive time will be transfigured through
the eternity of the Kingdom. The created universe will be both
abolished and fulfilled in the Kingdom as will be the unfolding
present, which provides structure to the universe. If time itself is a
creature, as we have naively suggested, it will not disappear. It will
instead realize its highest calling. Let us listen again to the Apocalypse: "In the middle of the square [of the celestial Jerusalem]
there is a tree that bears fruit twelve times, once for each month
of the year."[89] Does this not represent cyclical time, transfigured
by the explosion of the sun and the moon? This is neither the infernal wheel of destiny denounced by India nor the maelstrom of
life bewailed by St. Gregory of Nyssa. Freed from the barrenness
of winter, the tree becomes pure fecundity, pure life, a glorious simultaneity of permanent harvest, whose "leaves will heal the un-
believers." This is the eucharistic mystery of cosmic life become
again life-in-Paradise through the "tree of life planted in Calva-
ry,"[90] which is revealed to us in its fullness at the Second Coming.
The negation of the personal experience of time, expressed in
"there will be no more time," is offset by the correlative negation
"there will be no more death." The time abolished by eternity is
the bad time of separation. God will wipe the tears from their
eyes. "There will be no more death, there will be no more weep-
ing, no crying, no suffering, for the old world has passed away."[91]
By contrast, positive time, the time of love-engendering reciprocity, is found again in eternity, because eternity does not abolish

87. Revelation 22:3-4
88. Revelation 21:23
89. Revelation 22:3
90. Feast of the Exaltation of the Cross, Stichera of St. Andrew of Jerusalem.
91. Revelation 21:4

the personal but instead fulfills it. Eternity is not a swallowing up and dissolution into undifferentiation: it is the continuing new-ness of the encounter face to face.

We can now address the objections of those who say "this so-called linear time oriented toward God is no more, in sum, than a single cosmic cycle. You see less far than we do. Your bless-ed final state corresponds to the beginning of the cycle when all will recommence." Origen presented the Fathers with the same problem. According to Origen, the final state corresponded ex-actly to the initial state: the end and the beginning coincided. Things returned from immutability to immutability, restored by Christ. In his origin, man was a *noûs* contained in the Logos. There he was saturated in blessedness to the point of satiation and boredom. So he left to find something else and, through a process of condensation and cooling, became first soul and then body.[92]

Although Origen stresses the value of the experience that this trial yields, there is no guarantee that the cycle will not begin again, especially as change is the unique characteristic that distin-guishes man from God. If Origen went beyond Greek philosophy in his conception of freedom, he did not completely free himself from the cyclical conception of time or from nostalgia for a "de-finitive passage" at the limit. In their critique of Origen, the Cap-podocians challenged his metaphysical assumptions. They insist-ed on the radical ontological divide that separates the created from the uncreated. The created appears as an unfolding toward the uncreated, and this unfolding present is not abolished by eternity but instead expands into eternity. "Distance" persists in eternity. The created and the uncreated remain distinct and this fosters love without end. This is an infinite union, an end without end in which there can be neither "satiety" nor "passage to the limit." On the one hand there is the reality of the uncreated Creator, writes St. Grego-ry of Nyssa, "and on the other hand there is the reality of what was brought into existence through the creation. When creation turns toward its Creator, toward its first cause, it is, in a sense, continual-ly recreated and increased through the addition of goodness, with

---

92. Origen, *De Principiis*.

the result that the limits become invisible and growth becomes unconstrained."[93] The change from glory into glory, of which St. Paul speaks, and the longing for divine union are no doubt the most accurate image of the Kingdom, in which the best of time is found transformed by eternity. On the one hand, created nature is assimilated to the divine—this is *entasis*, seizure by longing, deification—everything that is conveyed by the prefix *epi*. On the other hand, the human person reaches (*ek*) lovingly toward the divine and the soul travels toward God through its own innerness. Time is thus transfigured into a perpetual "first time." "The soul fixes its eyes on the beauty of the bridegroom for the first time."[94] Eternity is not static uniformity: it is perpetually renewed wonder, an absolute beginning. "Those who climb never pause, going from beginnings without beginning through beginnings which have no end."[95] The time of the encounter and the time of love become eternal in a diverse unity, in which is revealed the inexhaustible secret of divine life that is the Trinity.

ΩΩΩ

If the meaning of time is to be found in divine *kenosis* and human freedom, in the encounter and finally the communion of God and man, it culminates in a single mystery, that of Christ and his Church. For the essence of the Church is the communion of God and man, and through this the communion of man and man, the communion of the blessed. The goal of creation is nothing less than the Church, or rather, the Church is already part of the divine project in the creative will that gives birth to the world.

"She is old," says the Shepherd of the woman who symbolizes the Church, "because she was created before all things and it was for her that the world was made."[96] In its liturgical texts

93. St. Gregory of Nyssa, *Song of Songs.*
94. Ibid.
95. St. Gregory of Nyssa, *Homily 8.*
96. Hermes, *The Shepherd*, Vision II.

the Orthodox Church depicts the first Church in Paradise, the Church of the Old Testament and even "the barren Church of Nations." Purified by divine pedagogy the Church of Israel bore fruit: it prepared the way for the "let it be" of Mary, that finally allowed God to become man, uniting the created and the uncreated. From that moment, man is summoned to become Church, to constitute by the grace of the Holy Spirit an "imitation" of the Trinity, in one Body of many persons.

One could say, so long as this boldness is not taken too literally, that the "Divine Council" or the "Council of the Saints" of the Trinity represent the eternal Church. God created, in order to give himself and to spread the life of love that radiates from the Trinity, in order to create the gift of the Church. It is the Church that reveals the mystery of the Trinity to men and to angels, the mystery "hidden from the ages in God."[97] It is one and the same act, at the limit of eternity and time, for God to create and to give himself. The creative act is enfolded in and guided by his will to give himself: God, the Church by nature, unites himself to mankind, the Church by grace. This is the sense of St. Paul's words "He chose us, in Christ, before the foundation of the world."[98] In this sentence, "before" does not mean chronologically anterior. It signifies God's plan in the moment before time in which he turns toward the birth-giving of time. It is God's "ideal will" (*idée-volonté*), his energy, that, in the instant at which time opens, causes providence to roll forth. And as this "ideal will" prepares and measures out how divine life is communicated to man, one could say that it is already the Church, the root, the center and the goal of history.

---

97. Ephesians 3:9
98. Ephesians 1:4

2. The Linear Time of the Old Covenant

According to Deuteronomy, the Israelites were to utter the following prayer when they offered the first fruits of the harvest to God:
"A wandering Aramean was my father; and he went down into
Egypt and sojourned there, few in number; and there he became
a nation, great, mighty, and populous. And the Egyptians treated
us harshly, and afflicted us, and laid on us hard bondage. Then
we cried to the Lord, the God of our fathers, and the Lord heard
our voice, and saw our affliction, our toil, and our oppression;
and the Lord brought us out of Egypt with a mighty hand and
an outstretched arm, with great terror, with signs and wonders;
and he brought us into this place and gave us this land, a land
flowing with milk and honey. And behold, now I bring the first
of the fruit of the ground, which thou, O Lord, hast given me."[99]
At this moment the cosmic offering became the sign of a faith
located in time: worship was no longer witness to the god of the
cosmos but to the God of history. The Bible as a whole is a sacred
history, the account of the great works of God, who intervenes
in and steps into history. The linear time of the Old Testament is
oriented toward an event whose meaning is constantly enriched
through successive trials: this is, as has been studied exhaustively,
the time of divine pedagogy. We will limit our analysis to showing how this revolution took place, replacing the cosmic rhythms
with those of hope and faith. In examining certain themes that
the Bible and archaic religions have in common, we shall see, for
example, how the biblical conception of the flood affirms the continuity of history; how the destruction of the Tower of Babel places a ban on all future attempts to conquer an impersonal eternity;
and how the archaic identification of the earth with the female
leads to the symbolism of marriage. Abraham's sacrifice of his son
allows us to observe as cosmic ritual is replaced by faith rooted in
history. Finally, the full new reality of biblical time becomes clear
as markers in time are victorious over markers in space and as
historical commemoration triumphs over the cosmic feast.

---

99. Deuteronomy 26:5-10

I.   The Flood and the Continuity of History

The universal theme of the flood almost always symbolizes a periodic destruction. Everything disappears and everything begins again, according to the rules of cyclical time. There is no historical continuity between the time before and after the flood. A mythical intermediary, whether god, demigod, or superhuman hero, gives rise to a completely new human race.[100]

The biblical story is quite different. While the presence of superhuman beings is certainly suggested in the giants of Genesis 6:4, their appearance seems to be the cause of God's wrath. They had been born as a result of a mysterious intermingling of angels and the daughters of men. Perhaps this passage in Genesis suggests that a Luciferian gnosis had emerged, giving prodigious powers to certain men, to "giants." Be that as it may, it is a man of the purest human lineage who survives the moment of the flood and preserves the continuity of both cosmic and human history. A man finds favor in the eyes of God because of his righteousness. The continuity of history is born of the encounter of the grace of God with the freedom of man. One man gives God the courage to see that his primordial design is still possible. For this reason, the Fathers have rightly seen the ark as a "type" of the Church. In God's plan the ark was already the Church. The flood's destruction was not the end of a cycle but a step in an ordered succession, or *acolouthia*, to use St. Gregory of Nyssa's terminology.

"After becoming subject to death through its propensity for sin, fallen humanity is no longer anchored in the good. Perfection cannot be regained in a single step, as was possible in Paradise. As it eliminates its contrary dispositions, humanity advances step by step toward the good, through order (*taxa*) and succession (*acolouthia*)."[101]

The flood is no more an interruption in the history of humanity than baptism, of which the flood is a "type," a disruption in the life of the individual. From this moment on, the cosmic

---

100. Eliade 2 §72
101. Gregory of Nyssa, *Song of Songs*, Homily 15.

order is no longer simply a manifestation of divine energy: it is the sign of God's personal promise and of his personal covenant and alliance with mankind.

II.   The Tower of Babel and the Axis of the World

The history of religion has shed light on the story of the Tower of Babel. The tower appears to have been one of the many ziggurats that were scattered across Mesopotamia as symbols of the "axis of the world." At Harsa, the ziggurat was called "the house of the joining of heaven and earth." At Babylon it was called "the link between heaven and earth" while at Borsippa it was called "the temple of the masters of heaven and earth." The steps of the ziggurat represented the ladder of contemplative life, whose steps the contemplative had to master methodically in order to become one with the axis of the world and to force open the gates of heaven.

Now the Living God destroyed the tower, the prototype of all ziggurats. And this destruction confirmed man's irrevocable loss, through the Fall, of the highway of the tree of life. Now mankind's nostalgia for Paradise, unless it were to become prayer and the expectation of redemption, could only end in usurpation and in the Luciferian desire to become God through one's own powers. Through his own forces, man cannot conquer sin, death, and the abyss between the created and the uncreated. The Tower of Babel is a tree shattered by lightning, rooted not in heaven but in the earth's will for power, and standing between the tree of life of Paradise and the new tree of life of the Cross.

The axis of the world is the symbol of an impersonal presence: it is a "totalization" of space that contains time within cyclical space. God's descending to destroy this axis is the expression of a personal and dynamic presence. This theophany is no longer a cosmic event but an event in history. The moment of destruction leads to a purification of history and to the mystery of the chosen people. Although tribes are henceforth scattered, one of them becomes the chosen people. It is surely significant that, following the description of the ruined tower, Genesis enumerates the ancestors of Abraham, among whom stands Eber, who will give his name to the Hebrews.

III. Mother Earth and Nuptial Symbolism

The Hebrews are to some degree inheritors of the cultural heritage of the Canaanites, but in the embrace of their God the Hebrews adopted and remade the fundamental image of agrarian religion, the identification of the earth with the feminine. "You shall no longer be termed Forsaken, and your land shall no longer be termed Desolate: but you shall be called 'my delight is in her' and your land 'Married.'"[102] There is a decisive difference of emphasis between this biblical conception and the old agrarian symbolism. Rather than being defined by her functional maternal role and symbolizing cosmic or metaphysical femininity, the woman takes on her personal reality as spouse. When applied to the earth and to people, the symbolism of the female therefore no longer leads to orgiastic ecstasy or to sacred prostitution but to the mystery of conjugal love. Orgiastic ecstasy seeks to intensify the moment in order to escape the languors of time, and both time and the person are negated as man is reduced to his sexual impulse. Conjugal love on the other hand replaces the momentary by time and duration and orgiastic eroticism by authentic love, the lucid discovery of a person through the embrace of nature.

Conjugal love implies an interplay of closeness and distance, of renewal and boredom, of knowledge and infidelity that joins it to a perpetually unfolding present, one whose goal is an eternal fulfillment.[103]

Conjugal symbolism is at once essentially personal and dramatic and at the same time eschatological. "To love someone," wrote Gabriel Marcel, "is to tell them 'you will not die.'" Love is therefore especially appropriate to describe the relationship be-

---

102. Isaiah 62:4-5
103. A. Neher, *L'Essence du Prophetisme*, Paris, 1955.

tween God and his people. Hosea expresses, in incomparable poetry, the tender nostalgia that fills the divine heart when the vision of the desert evokes in God the wonder of first love. Despite Israel's infidelity these moments return: "I will allure her, and bring her into the wilderness, and speak tenderly to her. And there I will give her vineyards, and make the Valley of Achor a door of hope. And there she shall answer as in the days of her youth, as at the time when she came out of the land of Egypt."[104]

This return is not nostalgia for Paradise or re-absorption into an eternal center: it is one step on a long conjugal history ravaged by human betrayal but illuminated by divine forgiveness. Unlike the automatic cycle of Greek or Indian philosophy, this return takes place through the instrument of time and eternity. The automatic cycle in Anaximander's system can be summarized as follows: "In being born, in detaching itself from the divine primordial unity in order to become that which it is now, matter has committed an act of extreme impiety for which it will suffer the supreme punishment of death and destruction."[105] Matter, therefore, perishes automatically and returns to the "divine primordial unity." And from there the cycle renews itself perpetually.

By contrast, the biblical return is accomplished through an act of free divine forgiveness: "for a brief moment I forsook you, but with great compassion I will gather you . . . In overflowing wrath for a moment I hid my face from you, but with everlasting love I will have compassion on you, says the Lord, your Redeemer."[106] A personal metaphysics of becoming takes the place of a mechanical philosophy of return, a becoming that unfolds toward the complete union of God and man, toward Christ, wholly God and wholly man, and toward his Church, in which the nuptial love of God and his people can finally be realized in each human person.

For this reason the Song of Solomon is without doubt the most important Old Testament text, proclaiming the mystery of divine love: the love of God and his people, of God and the

---

104. Hosea 2:14-15
105. Chestov, *Le Pouvoir des Clés*, p. 135.
106. Isaiah 54:5-8

Church, of God and the Christian soul, which, with the grace of the Holy Spirit, relives in person the long conjugal history of the Old Covenant, a history that Christ recapitulates and fills with definitive meaning.

IV.   The Sacrifice of Abraham: Faith Based in History Replaces Cosmic Ritual

The well-known story of Abraham and Isaac makes clear the difference between the archaic conception of ritual and archetypal repetition and the biblical conception of faith. This faith is not based on belief or loving fusion but is founded in one person's assent to a personal, divine presence, or for the time of the Old Testament it would be more accurate to say, to a personal, divine will. As Eliade so elegantly showed, the sacrifice of Abraham seems superficially to be no more than a specific instance of a widespread paleo-semitic ritual, the sacrifice of the first-born, who is often considered to be the child of God.[107] In the ancient East, young women would spend a night in the temple and the child thus conceived would be the child of God, a "stranger." The sacrifice of the first child—God's child—restores that which is his to the divinity, and ensures the flow of divine energy in the cosmos, from God to nature through fecundity, and from nature and man to God through sacrifice.

In a certain sense Isaac was indeed a child of God, as he had been miraculously given to Abraham and Sarah. But we should note a fundamental distinction. Isaac was given to his parents by the free choice of God, because of their faith, as the intervention of a personal God who upset the "laws of nature": this occurred through an act of faith rather than through the blind workings of natural laws. Likewise, although the sacrifice of Isaac is similar in form to other newborn sacrifices of the paleo-semitic world, it is wholly different in content. For the ancient Semitic peoples such a sacrifice was a ritual, a rationalized step-by-step invocation of

---

107. Eliade 1, pp. 161-164.

the supernatural; for Abraham sacrifice was an act of faith. Ritual sacrifice had a very clear meaning for those offering it: sacrifice was one element of a logical and coherent system which animated the cosmos. To use Kierkegaard's terminology, sacrifice formed part of the *general*. By contrast, Abraham did not understand why this sacrifice was required of him and yet he carried it out, with complete trust in the God who demanded it of him. The God of Abraham is metalogical: he is personal. He transcends the category of the *general*. Still more, he transcends anticipation. The paleo-semitic sacrifice is repetition of an archetype. It is carried out with the gaze fixed on a mythical past that is the basis and guarantee of its effectiveness. Abraham's trust looks to the future. God's order destroys the present without rendering the present meaningless, because God contains all future possibilities. God tests Abraham. He tests Abraham's faith so that it should become rooted in God alone and not in human means, even if those were given by God. The sacrifice demanded of Abraham, the sacrifice of the object of all his hope and of the promise of an inheritor, required unconditional obedience and a faith beyond logic. It is no longer a question of seeing divine energy made transparent in the cosmos. There is a relationship between two persons that transcends and even ignores nature. When Abraham's son questions him as they climb the mountain, Abraham answers, "God himself will provide the lamb for a burnt offering, my son."[108] At the last moment God replaces the human victim with a ram: in this moment it becomes clear that each time man obeys God, the Lamb of God is lifted up. If a man has offered God his own son, how can God not give his own Son to mankind?

We see here how the Old Testament is not just the history of divine intervention and the prefiguration of salvation. It is also the history of man's refusal and acceptance. God's expectation and waiting, his disappointments and his gifts, are also a mystery. "What more was there to do for my vineyard, that I have not done to it? When I looked for it to yield grapes, why did it yield wild

---

108. Genesis 22:8

grapes?"[109] Salvation draws near or draws away, according to a person's readiness or not to welcome the *kairos* of Christ. Salvation depends not only on a divine decision but also on human willingness. The Annunciation and the Virgin's "let it be according to thy will" are both required in order to untangle the tragic web of human freedom.

In the Old Testament justice is defined in relation to history rather than in relation to the cosmos. It is no longer a question of following the laws of the cosmos, whether of the Greek cosmos or the Hindu dharma. Old Testament justice requires faithfulness to the divine command, whence its personal character. As Bultmann noted, Marcus Aurelius's advice to "consider the nature of the whole" is of no value here.[110] Man cannot free himself from his suffering by depersonalizing it, by considering himself to be merely one unimportant aspect of the universal order. Man is in a state of becoming before God and must look for everything in the future, that is to say, from God alone.

V.   The Temporal Sign Gains Priority over the Spatial Symbol, the Future over the Past

There is no shortage of symbolism of cosmic space in the Bible. The Psalms and the Book of Job celebrate divine wisdom and glory as revealed in the splendor of creation. "Ask the beasts and they will teach you and the fish of the sea will declare unto you."[111] But as the biblical narrative proceeds, time gains in significance over space, and the temporal sign gains over the spatial symbol. What counts most for the prophets is the sudden unveiling of God's will through an apparently accidental chain of events, summoning the prophet's attention: this is altogether different from matter as unspeaking witness or the decoding of the immanent universe through the parable or *maschal*. Jeremi-

---

109. Isaiah 5:4
110. Bultmann, *Primitive Christianity*, Paris, 1950. Citing Marcus Aurelius, *Pensées*.
111. Job 12:7-8

ah had many times watched farmers burning straw under the cauldron. But suddenly he stands before a cauldron that is tipping toward the south. While any cauldron can accidentally take on a symbolic meaning, here we see a direct transcendental intervention that makes use of the object—the cauldron—to evoke a historical menace, the Chaldean invasion that will deploy from the north.

"'What do you see?' And I said, 'I see a bubbling pot and it is tipped from the North.' Then the Lord said: 'Out of the North evil shall break forth upon the inhabitants of the land.'" And again, "the word of the Lord came to me, saying 'Jeremiah, what do you see?' And I said, 'I see a rod of almond*.' Then the Lord said to me, 'You have seen well, for I am watching* over my word to perform it.'" [112]

We see here the sign of divine faithfulness rather than the symbol of the return of spring. The cosmos serves only to make clear the meaning of the divine word. The cosmic is no longer a manifestation but instead has become the fortuitous instrument of a transcendent intervention, pure contingency used in the instant by God to break into history.

Likewise, the agrarian festivals are transformed after the Exodus from primitive celebrations of a cosmic liturgy to memorials of God's work. Passover, the festival of spring, which marked the beginning of the barley harvest, becomes a remembrance of the departure from Egypt. Pentecost, the festival of summer, the bringing in of the wheat harvest, becomes the celebration of the promulgation of the Law on Sinai, fifty days after the crossing of the Red Sea. And the autumn festival of the tabernacles, which marked the end of the wine harvest, becomes the remembrance of the huts built by the people as they traveled through the desert. "And so the God to whom Israel offers the first-born of its flock and the first fruits of its harvest is no longer a faceless divinity from which mysterious life forces arose: it is Yahweh, the God of our fathers, who had taken them out from under Pharaoh's tyr-

---

112. Jeremiah 1:13 Translation adapted from the Anchor Bible, *Jeremiah*, ed. Bright, 1965. The * designates a Hebrew pun on *shaqed* and *shoqed*.

anny. *In becoming historical remembrance the liturgy is stamped with the personal traits of God.*"[113]

One might imagine that this liturgy of remembrance would have turned the chosen people toward the past. Nothing of the kind happened. God's triumphant intervention served as a guarantee of his protection now and in the future. Every form of slavery was seen in the light of the subjection in Egypt, to the extent that the commemoration of the Exodus was transformed into the promise of a new Exodus. Isaiah suggests that the destruction of the Assyrians will be a new Passover: "God will protect Jerusalem and deliver it, he will spare and rescue it."[114] In the liturgical remembrance, the prophets discern the future actions of God. The events of the Exodus, God's intervention once and for all, make clear God's sovereignty over history for all future generations.[115]

The Old Testament reveals history as theophany. This history is one of the chosen people being repeatedly invited and falling away. Each time, God saves a remnant whose faithful vigil is purified by the successive disappointments. The waiting for the triumphant Messiah becomes the waiting of the suffering servant of Yahweh; the expectation of the political liberation of the people becomes the expectation of the spiritual liberation of mankind. At least this is the case for the true "remnant," the "poor of Israel," the remnant that is also a seedbed. The prophets rooted out any reassuring conception of the covenant: they showed that the covenant was based not on the regular fulfillment of the required cult worship but on individual ethical fidelity and penitence. Therefore no one can rely on the fact of an alliance concluded in the past. The alliance becomes the heart of Israel's and of each Israelite's existence. No one can count on the fact of being one of the chosen people to guarantee their own security: the fate of their election depends on each person's response to God's commandments. At the same time, the liturgy becomes an inner event. The events of the Exodus are transformed in the Psalms into inner,

113. J. Gillet, *Thèmes Bibliques*, Paris, 1954, pp. 10-11 (italics in original).
114. Isaiah 31:5
115. Gillet, ibid.

spiritual events. For the true remnant and seedbed of Israel, the idea of the alliance becomes at once personal and eschatological, the long-awaited Exodus, a definitive liberation accomplished by crossing the waters of death.

The Psalm rises up, praying that God who was the shepherd of the ancestors in the desert will now become the Good Shepherd: "For he is our God, and we are the sheep of his pasture and the flock of his hand. Today, be attentive to his voice."[116] And God responds in the words of the prophet:

"Behold, the days are coming, says the Lord, when I will make a new covenant with the house of Israel and the house of Judah, not like the covenant which I made with their fathers when I took them out by the hand to bring them out of the land of Egypt, my covenant which they broke, though I was their husband, says the Lord. But this is the covenant which I will make with the house of Israel after those days, says the Lord: I will put my law within them, and I will write it upon their hearts; and I will be their God and they shall be my people. And no longer shall each man teach his neighbor and his brother, saying, 'know the Lord,' for they shall all know me, from the least of them to the greatest, says the Lord; for I will forgive their iniquity, and I will remember their sin no more."[117]

VI. Conclusion: The Time of Great Expectation, the Time of Penitential Preparation

"A voice cries: In the wilderness prepare the way of the Eternal, make straight in the desert a highway for our God. Every valley shall be lifted up, and every mountain and hill be made low; the uneven ground shall become level, and the rough places a plain. And the glory of the Lord shall be revealed, and all flesh shall see it together, for the mouth of the Lord has spoken."[118]

---

116. Psalm 94:7
117. Jeremiah 31:31-34
118. Isaiah 40:3-5 (RSV) Adapted to reflect the author's use of "the Eternal."

The whole significance of linear time, straining toward something not as yet accomplished, will be summed up in the prophecy of John the Baptist: "Repent, for the kingdom of Heaven is near."[119] But the Kingdom has not yet come. The linear time of the Old Testament is no longer part of the cyclical return but it is not yet the Christian communion. It is the time of the nocturnal confrontation between man and God—the same confrontation that won Jacob the name of Israel. The holiness of the Old Testament is not yet the free deification of man. The faithful and just man can become the instrument of divine will; he prepares himself to serve, with a faith not yet made clear, through obedience and purity of heart. These are negative concepts. Obedience and purity of heart imply the externality of God and man's submission as God's instrument. The Spirit descends on the prophets; God makes use of man as his instrument, imposing himself from outside the person. The unseen God speaks: his servant listens. The darkness of Sinai and the light of Mount Tabor stand as the two poles of the veiled and unveiled mystery. "The Glory that once overshadowed the tabernacle and spake with Thy servant Moses, O Master, was a figure of Thy Transfiguration that ineffably shone forth as lightning upon Tabor."[120] There is a crushing inequality between man and God: man does not participate in divine life and the transcendent monad is constantly on the verge of destroying his creation, man. The God of the Old Testament is the God of the storm who, when touched by human sin, manifests his love as rage. Cosmic catastrophes are the direct result of human catastrophes, summoning man to repentance.

In their intensity, God's holiness and loving-kindness appear as incomprehensible manifestations of the All-Powerful, and remain external to man, whose world of sin and death cannot bear their contact. Job is silent and repents when faced with the whims of the all-powerful master of Leviathan and Behemoth. But the God who obtained Job's silent submission and prostration and who returned to him the same number of children as

---

119. Matthew 3:2
120. Matins for the Transfiguration, Troparion of the 3rd ode of the 2nd Canon.

had been taken away—as though it was a matter of the loss of wealth and not the loss of irreplaceable beings—the God who maintained his silence in response to Job's questions, is in the end a God who did not and has not yet replied.

And so there are two contradictory impasses that are resolved only in the Incarnation, as is still true today outside of Christ. In archaic religion and in Eastern metaphysics, divine energy is indeed revealed by the cosmic rhythms, and man by his existence participates in the outpouring of divine life, but the personal intimacy of this divine life is not within man's reach. In this case participation in the divine precludes love, because love can only flow between two persons. God is robbed of personhood in the manifestation of divine nature through the natural world and the cosmos, while the personhood of man is threatened by dissolution through *entasis* or through orgy. Conversely, in today's Islam and Judaism, the religions of Abraham, God's personal reality is revealed, but this personal God is, as it were, enclosed within his transcendent sovereignty. The depths of divine love are locked within his monad and he remains exterior to both man and the cosmos.[121] Nature is desanctified; man cannot see God without dying; God is in heaven and man is on earth.[122]

Cyclical time seeks to be reabsorbed into eternity: the result is to confound time and space and to depersonalize both God and man. Linear time isolates man from nature and from God: this is submission in an empty world to a fearsome God. The cyclical time of the sacred cosmos is immersion into a unity without diversity. The linear time of the Old Testament is confrontation without unity, the tragic duality of man and God.

The Incarnation, breaking into time, reveals the profundity of the eternal Trinity. A divine Person of the Trinity comes to restore our nature by joining human and divine nature in a perfect unity. This is the resolution of the double impasse, the double

---

121. Mysticism seeks to break through this impasse, but only succeeds at the cost of falling into the other impasse, dissolution and depersonalization. The Cabbala and late Sufism are transfixed on the horns of this dilemma. Mansur al-Hallaj was executed for his attempt to find a middle way.

122. Exodus 34:20; Ecclesiastes 5:2.

set of expectations with which man had wrestled lucidly in linear time and which he had sought to resolve through nostalgia in cyclical time. When Mary said to the angel, "Behold the handmaid of the Lord; let it be according to thy word,"[123] the double time of waiting is resolved. On the one hand this has been the vigil of human history, the vigil for the moment in which God is finally able to enter into the unfolding present, not through the crushing intervention of the storm and the thunderbolt, in which man remains merely an instrument, but through consent freely given.

Mary's ancestors, blessed by God and purified by the Law, received the words of the Logos in their soul; as the summation of their sanctity Mary receives the Logos himself in the very intimacy of her being. But Mary's "let it be" is also a response to the nostalgia for cosmic cycles. It resolves not only the drama of human freedom (history) but also the drama of natural rhythms perpetually defending life against death and bringing forth life from death. Through the Virgin, earthly flesh at last gives birth, not to a being subject to death, but to the definitive resurrection. For this reason, the veneration of the Theotokos, while using expressions that undoubtedly derive from the archaic worship of the Earth-Mother, is in no way a pagan corruption of Christianity: it is rather one aspect of Christianity's profound truth. The coming of Christ is not only exorcism and judgment; it is also fulfillment. It places the seal of the whole truth on the partial truths to which the universal cosmic rhythms witness. The first truly "deified" human person, the Virgin, is also the first who fully *enhypostasizes* the terrestrial world. Through her is found the meaning of the beauty, the fruitfulness, and the cosmic wisdom which were the objects of archaic worship. Mary takes into her being all the life of the world in order to purify it and to make it an offering. In the profound image of St. Irenaeus, she is the earth become once again virgin soil so that God could fashion from it the New Adam.[124]

---

123. Luke 1:38 (RSV)
124. St. Irenaeus, *Against the Heresies.*

3.   The Economy of the Son:
the Liberation and the Recapitulation of Time

St. Cyril of Alexandria explored in depth the *kenosis* of the Son.[125]
In becoming incarnate, it was impossible for God to have shed
his own nature, for he would have no longer have been God, and
then one could not speak of the Incarnation. The subject of kenosis is therefore not the divine nature but the human person of the
Son. The person is fulfilled in self-abandonment. This is why, as
St. Paul wrote, the Son did not count equality with God a thing
to be grasped, but emptied himself in the form of a servant. Here
the person is distinguished from the divine nature in an act of
perfect renunciation, and this renunciation is itself the most perfect manifestation of his existence as person.[126] That is to say it is
neither an exogenous decision, alien to the Son, nor is it an act of
his own will; it is his very hypostatic reality, a total self-giving to
the will of the Trinity; the will of which the Father is the source,
the Son is the obedient realization, and the Spirit is the glorious
fulfillment. There is therefore an intimate continuity between the
personal existence of the Son and his *kenosis*: between the gift of
the Son to the Father and the Holy Spirit and his coming into the
time of here below.

For Christ-become-man, time is precisely the measure
of his total receptiveness to all that comes from the Father. For
Christ, temporal existence was the most perfect means of trans-
lating the vital movement, the personal aspect, of his eternity.
Time, for Christ, was self-giving through the Holy Spirit to the
will of the Father, a succession in which, through the Spirit, the
coming instant is a gift that cannot be anticipated. (Adam, by
contrast, attempted to accelerate time and to anticipate the will of
his Creator by grasping the tree of life.) For Christ, to be in time is
to receive it in its uniqueness from the hand of God, so that each
instant belongs to God. Even the Son does not know the hour and
desires to receive it unheralded from the Father.

---

125. Lossky, pp. 140-141.
126. Philippians 2:5-11

In this way the Incarnation reveals to us the meaning of time: time is the possibility of self-giving (abandon) and of love. If God has subjected sinful man to death it is in order to compel him, despite everything, to self-giving and abandon. It follows therefore that even the baneful aspects of fallen time are a crucible for the revelation of time as the mystery of love brought to us by the Incarnation. Time is the reflection of divine life, of the communion of three Persons. As Oscar Cullmann demonstrated, the opposition of time and eternity is done away with. For eternity is not some thing but some one, or more precisely it is the life in love of the three Persons of the Trinity. In the created being (created, let us not forget, in the image of God) life transmits and admits the dynamism of one person toward another, that human dynamism that is the giving of oneself to one's neighbor and to God.

In the encounter in time with the "other," the "other" can never be fully known in his essence and can never be objectified. The dynamism of love born in time, giving time its meaning, requires eternal life for its fulfillment. This was indeed the divine project since the creation: to give time to man as the passage from self to other, so that he would not be trapped within himself but would launch himself toward the supreme other. A deep longing remains after the Fall, the deep longing of the Song of Solomon, the longing of a love that is stronger than death. And so time reaches its fullness through the Resurrection of the Son of Man: a moment of complete emptiness is joined at last in an act of free and total self-giving and is transformed into the moment of complete fulfillment. Eternal life is not the monotony of the solitary monad, but is communion in him who is not alone in himself. For this reason the love of the Trinity can flow into time, revealing its true meaning.

Its most profound meaning is this: time was not made for death but for eternity. Time was created not to destroy and be destroyed but to expand into eternal life. Death entered the world with the first lie, when man chose freely to listen to the serpent; when he willingly assented to the offer of a beautiful reality outside of God's command; when he set up a system of autonomous values, in which the only measure of man was man. In this way

man separated himself from the source of life and this separation came to be carved into time itself in the form of usury, destruction, and death. For both man and his environment nature
was created as transparency, as openness, as the vital urge toward
eternity. Nature now finds itself bound to the laws of corruption
and death. Nature has become anti-nature, because the true nature of man is the fullness of life in unity with God.

Each death is a hit carried out by the one "who was a mur-
derer from the beginning."[127] Man and the universe, through man,
are prisoners of death, enslaved to the cycles of a life that can only
engender death. This is why God came to deliver man from his
prison, to offer him the possibility of complete life. He enters the
kingdom of the dead in order to conquer death. For Christ temporal existence is a descent into hell, into suffering piled on suffering, leading to the night in Gethsemane and the ascent to Gol-
gotha. Christ always carried with him time in its purest form. His
human nature was deified from the moment of his conception,
as is shown by his miraculous birth. The body that is born from
the flesh of Mary is the same body that after the Resurrection will
pass through walls and will play with space and fallen time: it will
play with the separation of time and space that gives substance to
man's separated condition as sinner. Christ opens the possibility
of the deification of time to those within fallen time: in time he
walked on the water, in time he was transfigured. In obedience
to the Father, he voluntarily shared all our poverty and he alone
tapped the full depths of fallen time. "In traveling the roads of
life, O Savior, you voluntarily went hungry, desiring the salvation
of all; for the hunger that you felt is the desire for the return of
all who have fallen away far from you."[128] We consider it normal
to consume the flesh of this world instead of transfiguring it into
an offering to God. We have seized the world and sunk our teeth
into it. We have upended the hierarchy of creation, in which the

---

127. John 8:44
128. 8th Ode Compline, Great and Holy Monday, St. Andrew of Crete. Translator's note: Clément's reference does not correspond to the cited text in the
Faber Lenten Triodion.

higher should nourish the lower by sanctifying it: the spirit for the soul, the soul for the body, the body for the earth. Instead, the higher quells its hunger for absolute power in ceaselessly devouring the lower; the spirit feeds off the aspirations of the soul; the soul is nourished by bodily passions; the body is consumed by and consumes the world, killing in order to eat, until the day the earth closes over his lifeless corpse.

In Christ the spirit, the soul, and the body have resumed their original place, a place of service. The Body of Christ is a body that gives life, a body that does not kill but is the bread of life. That is why this body alone could know the terrible anguish of hunger and thirst. For us everything is confused: our body is completely subject to the rhythms of hunger and thirst—that is the norm of our fallen condition. For Christ, the body was first and foremost an openness in time to the will of the Father, a fire of love that melted the laws of nature "congealed" in sin, and, adding to the miracle, restored beings and matter to their true nature, to their vocation of adoration. He who resurrected the dead accepted death. Not that he had to die like us as the necessary development of an unnatural condition, as the tragic fruit of sin, but as pure obedience to the Father. His descent into our incompleteness is striking: he had so simply brought back to life the son of the widow of Nain and Jairus's daughter, as if it were a game. Yet he trembled before the tomb of Lazarus and he sweated blood in the Garden of Gethsemane. His crucifixion was an inconceivable rending apart. He had taken the full measure of what man had made of time: the fascination with non-existence and the flight from God. He, *the one who alone should not die*,[129] had sounded the abyss of separated humanity, the abyss of death, with his transfigured humanity. Death is the undertow of our fallen existence. Life itself was the measure of the Second Adam's obedience and adoration. We are within death. He descended into death, who himself was a stranger to death. His death took the full measure of all human death, of all human deaths; it summed up and destroyed the reality of death.

---

129. Translator's note: italics in original.

When the Bread of Life submits to hunger, when the Source of Life submits to thirst, when the Living Transfigured Man submits to death, everything is changed; all is turned upside down. Hunger, thirst, and death now become openings to life. He reveals to us the meaning of our hunger and gives himself to us as food. He reveals to us the meaning of our thirst and gives himself to us as drink. He reveals to us the meaning of our death and resurrects us with himself. Because hunger, thirst, death, and the hell that believed it had a mortal in its grasp have met the God-Man: in him, in the fiery abyss of his divinity, the abyss of death is vaporized like an insignificant droplet of hate: "Hell took a body and met God face to face . . . Christ is risen, and not one dead remains in the grave."[130]

This is the kerygma: "Christ is risen, trampling down death by death." We are each the Samaritan woman but as one illuminated by Pentecost. Christ has revealed to us the meaning of our thirst. The water that we drink does not merely sustain a life that is bound to death: "He who drinks of the water that I shall give shall not thirst for evermore."[131] This is an inverted sacrament—a communication of death. But Christ reveals to us that we wish to drink all of life and that he alone can bring us this life, because it is the eternal flowing forth of the spring of the Trinity, the flowing forth of the fullness of God. For this reason he, truly God and truly man, offers himself to us as "living water": "the water I shall give him will turn within him into a spring of water jetting up into eternal life."[132] "He who eats my flesh and drinks my blood has life everlasting."[133]

Our fallen existence in time, assumed by the Lord even into the depths of hell, is transformed into deified time. Living water flows henceforth from the cracks of fragmented non-being. In our hands the cross is the magician's wand that causes living water to flow. If through our faith we identify the instant of our

---

130. St. John Chrysostom, *Pascal Homily*, text from *The Pascal Service*, Orthodox Church in America, 2004.
131. John 4:13
132. John 4:14
133. John 6:54

death with the passage on the cross, that moment on the cross comes alive. Beneath the superficial flux and indifference of life are depths not only of anguish, but beyond anguish, of joy. The time of Paradise has passed from life to the Living One, fallen time has passed from life to death, the time that is offered to us by Christ passes, through death, from life to Life.

Paradisaical time was fragile and the freedom that it offered to man contained the hidden risk of death. The time offered to us by Christ has a hidden stability: our crimes are already pardoned and all that is asked of us is repentance and humility. "Lord Jesus Christ, Son of God, have mercy on me, a sinner." It is true that we continue to die: Christ could not, for his chosen people, break the great ties of solidarity that link all men through death. Nor could he impose himself through triumphant victory, risking stifling human freedom and sterilizing the mystery of faith. Christ himself conquered death by death. Each of us also will die, but this death, which is with us at every moment, will transform the unnatural separation of body and soul into a supreme metamorphosis, a letting go in faith, the entry into a state of peace and purification, in which the soul prepares to clothe itself in the body of a transfigured Cosmos, in the singleness of an unconfused Tri-Unity. Death signifies annihilation: not as the acquiring of non-being, which would be a contradiction in terms, but as the shrinking away of that part of being that is non-being, a reduction that is always in process and yet never fully accomplished. Apart from God, the immortality of the soul is no more than a phantom existence.

This is the sense in which death no longer exists for the Christian. He has already died in Christ and resurrected with him through baptism. Baptism is our real birth because our physical birth is into a world that is subject to death. "What is born of the flesh is flesh"[134] (and here flesh denotes the mortal world) whereas our new birth in the Spirit, that joins us to the life of the resurrection, opens to us a life that is without ending, a life that penetrates and transforms mortal life, even while coming to us through

---

134. John 3:6

mortal life. Therefore physical death gives way to an ascetic process of dying to death, of becoming alive through the shedding of
our mortal flesh. This alone makes us capable of loving and transfiguring the mortal nature from which we free ourselves. In Orthodox asceticism, ecstasy is merely a transitional stage that must
be passed through in order to accomplish the metamorphosis of
the body and of the earth. Death appears as ecstasy that prepares
man for the new heaven and the new earth.

For those who are perfect, for those who before their physical death have known that instant of anguish and wonder in
which the grace of baptism is made real, for those who worked in
the very heart of time for its metamorphosis, of whom the Gospels and St. Paul speak, for these death is an almost unnoticeable
step that does not interrupt their work. Among the dead who are
plunged into a purifying ecstasy that has the appearance of sleep,
the prayers of the martyrs at the celestial altar lighten the burden
of human history and work in communion with those laboring
on earth for the building of the Kingdom of God.

ΩΩΩ

*"That everything in Heaven and on earth should be
summed up in Christ"*[135]

The cyclical time of nature and the historical time of the
Covenant contract into, or in the words of St. Paul, are recapitulated in, Christ. St. Irenaeus comments on this at length.[136] St.
John says everything came about through the Word.[137] The Epistle to the Hebrews tells us, "God who in ancient times spoke to
our fathers in many and various ways through the prophets, has

---

135. Ephesians 1:10
136. *Against the Heresies*
137. John 1:3

now in these last days spoken to us through his Son."[138] As the Fathers often noted there is, as it were, a triple incarnation of the Word, in the cosmos, in sacred history, and in Jesus Christ. But the full incarnation is no longer just the manifestation of divine energy: it is the becoming human of the second Person of the Trinity, revealing the full meaning of the first two incarnations. Or rather, there is a single incarnation, the third, which draws in and transfigures all human and cosmic reality and makes it possible to read the presence of the Word in the bible of the natural world. Without the Incarnation the *logoï* of matter and the Word of the Old Testament would remain incomprehensible to us, as if written in an unknown language. Only the gift of tongues at Pentecost enables us to understand Christ's twofold message: "Lift up your eyes and see the fields already white for the harvest. The Word in the presence of his disciples warns those who listen to lift up their eyes to the field of Scripture and to the fields of the Word that is in every being, so as to see the radiant whiteness and splendor of the truth that is all around us."[139]

Christ is the new Adam, the last Adam, come to restore creation once and for all. Taking on human destiny he perfects all that is positive in creation and history and destroys all that is negative—or rather, he changes its polarity and makes it a container of life. By his ministry he fulfills the example and the expectation of the elect, of the patriarchs, of the lawmakers, and of the prophets. Through his solitude and exclusion he redeems the rejected, whose number has increased even as the life of the chosen people has advanced, and prepares the way for universal salvation. Through his transfiguration he perfects the theophanies of old. Through his death and Resurrection he destroys the empire of death that was established through the Fall. Thus summing up in himself both nature and history, he inaugurates a new creation, in which there is no longer any barrier separating human and divine nature.

---

138. Hebrews 1:2
139. Origen, *Commentary on St. John.*

The typological exegesis of the Fathers, incorporated into the Liturgy of the Church, teaches us that Christ reveals the Old Testament to be both the time of preparation of the kerygma and one dimension of the Incarnation: the words of the Law and the prophets are brought to fruition in the Gospels.[140] Let us cite only the handful of examples explored by Père de Lubac.[141] Christ is the true Noah, the architect of the ultimate Ark, the Church, which alone will survive the new flood, in which the whole universe will be baptized by fire. When the Bible tells us that Joshua, who bears the name of the Savior and shares his destiny, conquered the whole earth, this is not just hyperbole designating the conquest of Palestine; it is also the prophecy of the universal victory of the Good News. If the Hebrews went up from Egypt in forty-eight stages, this is because the Son of God descended to us, in the Egypt of this world, through the forty-eight steps of his ancestors in the flesh. The wood that sweetens the bitter water is an image of the cross. Abraham and Isaac climbing to the place of sacrifice are together an image of Christ as both priest and victim of the sacrifice. In Leviticus, almost every sacrificial offering presents an aspect of the ultimate sacrifice of the cross, in which all was recapitulated. The cross is "the perfect sacrifice of which all others are antitypes and images."[142]

In passing through Egypt, the desert, and the Jordan, Christ recapitulates the journey of Israel. His temptation, which puts an end to unfaithfulness, recapitulates that of Adam and of the Israelites in the desert. Israel demanded meat and was rewarded with quail.[143] Israel asked for a sign at Massa.[144] Israel worshiped the golden calf. Christ's rebuttals to Satan make him and his Church the true Israel from that moment on.

As "truly man" Christ recapitulates human history. If the biblical genealogies show him as son of David, son of Abraham, son of Adam, it is only because he was already present in them,

---

140. Origen, *Commentary on the Gospel of St. Matthew.*
141. Origen, Introduction, *Homily on the Exodus,* SC 16.
142. Origen, *Homily on Leviticus.*
143. Numbers 11:23
144. Exodus 17:2-7

and they in him, as partakers of his glorified humanity. As truly God—the Lord, *Kyrios*—he is the continuation of the interventions of Yahweh. He recapitulates divine history. Re-creation corresponds to creation; the taking on of flesh corresponds to the tabernacle; the new alliance corresponds to the old; the destruction of death corresponds to the Exodus.

Typology is not just a game of images: it is an expression of real participation. The tragic duality of the insignificance of man and the omnipotence of God is abolished. The elder of the Apocalypse announces "the lion from the tribe of Judah" and sees "a lamb, standing like one that has been slaughtered."[145] The time of sovereign intervention by the divine Monad is revealed as the painful time of expectation "since the establishment of the world" for the Lamb that was slain,[146] for a sacrifice that is written into history. The monadic deity is revealed in the Trinity as the immensity of love. Divine anger is shown to be love, rejected love, love powerless before the errant freedom of man, love in waiting, until finally there is a woman who is able to and wills to welcome it in. "The Incarnation is not only the work of the Father, His strength and His Spirit: it is also the work of the will and the faith of the Virgin."[147] The hand that sealed Job's lips is the hand that is now pierced. The pierced hand that lets the cry of suffering humanity penetrate to eternity, there to be consumed by love, is the true response to Job.[148] The celestial witness, who vouches for Job on high, whom Job at one moment dared to invoke, is brought down lower than Job in order to open the ecstatic love of the Trinity to those who invoke him.

ΩΩΩ

---

145. Revelation 5:5-6
146. Revelation 13:8
147. N. Cabasilas, *Patrologia Orientalis*, XIX.
148. Job 2:6, 16:19

If Christ recapitulates human history, he also gives the cosmic cycles their full meaning. The Fathers followed up on Philo's suggestion that all the cosmic symbolism of Greek religion could be assumed into the worship of a personal God. Seeing paganism fatally wounded and unable to break the new faith, they did not hesitate to give a Christian meaning to the cycles of nature. This has nothing to do with hyper-allegorical interpretation. It is the deciphering of the cosmic presence of the Lord, starting from the revelation of his hypostatic presence. As St. Augustine wrote, the revelation of Christ is given to us as "another world," that allows us to rediscover the meaning of this world, of the "first book of life."[149]

First and foremost, the diurnal rhythms: the paradisaical nostalgia for the "first sun on that first morning," the Egyptian symbolism of the "midnight sun," the sun that never sets of the Upanishads—these are all so many figures of Christ the Sun, so dear to Eusebius who saw therein the true victorious Christ of the Christian Empire. The sun-worship of the third century, on the other hand, represented paganism's supreme last effort to defeat the new religion. Christ is the sun who rises over the new creation, and over the liturgy of the cosmos. He is the "sun of justice [who] will rise, with healing in his wings."[150] He is the East, whence came the glory of God.[151] Dawn is universally clothed in the archaic symbolism of resurrection and the victory of life, the triumph of day over the forces of darkness. This symbolism is given its definitive meaning in the Song of Zechariah, who names Christ "the day-spring from on high" that has risen "to give light to them that sit in darkness, and in the shadow of death."[152]

> "The evening strips each man bare
> stretching him out for sleep
> and showing him that all he owns
> stays here below.

---

149. On Psalm 8:8, *De Trinitate*; 1.2.1, *Confessions*.
150. Malachi 3:20 (New Jerusalem Bible, adapted)
151. Ezekiel 43:2 (New Jerusalem Bible, adapted)
152. Luke 1:78-79 (BCP, adapted)

The evening strips off his garments,
leaving him naked
just as death strips man bare.
The morning appears . . .
The image of the Resurrection
extraordinary wonder.
A hymn to you, O my Savior,
who separates the night from the day
and makes them images,
mystical parables."[153]

Therefore "we should pray in the morning so that Christ's resurrection is celebrated through our morning prayer" and "when the sun sets and the day ends we should again pray. Christ is our true sun and our true light: when the sun goes down and the light of the world fades, we call on Christ's coming that brings the grace of eternal light."[154] The cycle of day and night, henceforth bathed in the light of Christ, who came and who will come again, is therefore for us the symbol of the "day without end" and of the "day which has no night." And so our daily prayer becomes "an imitation of what we one day ought to become."

"If in the Scriptures, Christ is called the true sun and the true light, then as Christians we cannot let a single hour pass without worshiping God in all places and at all times. Because we are in the light of the sun that is Christ, we should keep ourselves in prayer all day long. And when in the natural progression of things night returns, its darkness can do no harm to those who pray: they are the sons of light. For them daylight shines even in the darkness. He whose bright sun is named Christ is never deprived of sunshine and clarity."[155]

The victory over death becomes victory over night. Night, which notably is not mentioned at the time of the creation, is inserted into the fabric of time like an image of death.[156] Like death,

---

153. Syriac Hymn, quoted in *Dieu est Vivant*, No. 25.
154. St. Cyprian of Carthage
155. St. Cyprian of Carthage
156. "and there was evening and there was morning, a fourth day" (Genesis 1:19)

night has the merit of compelling man to renounce his semblance of autonomy and to abandon himself, to put his trust in sleep, to recharge his strength in sleep. "You gave us sleep as rest for our weakness and as relief from its many sufferings for our tired flesh."[157] Night is good, but also fearsome, the sign of the darkness of non-being introduced by man into creation. "But Judas took the crust and went out at once. *Now it was night.*"[158]

By his Resurrection in the heart of darkness Christ has changed the meaning of night. Night has become the container of a new light that knows no setting, of a luminous life freed from death. That is why "now that we have come to the setting of the sun and behold the light of evening" we "praise thee in voices of song."[159] Physical night becomes as it were the sacrament of the nuptial night, when the Bridegroom, already secretly present amidst the darkness, drives it away so that we are face to face with perfect joy. The Christian cannot for this reason sleep like the others in the unconsciousness of death or in the nightmare of passion. He holds vigil and his vigil is eschatological. "Behold, the Bridegroom comes in the middle of the night and happy the man who will be found waiting."[160] And even when he closes his eyes he prays that his heart will remain vigilant:

"Let my sleep be always filled with your presence.
Even when separated from the body
the spirit hymns You, O God."[161]

Yuletide, at the winter solstice, is a crying out in the darkness at the exact moment at which light is dawning. The Resurrection coincides with springtime. Through the symbolism willed for us by God, spring is the moment of the triumph of life, not merely for an ephemeral summer but for the eternal summer of the Kingdom. As Philo noted, the rebirth of nature at springtime marks the anniversary of creation, because accord-

---

157. Prayer of St. Basil, Midnight Office.
158. John 13:30
159. The ancient hymn "O Gladsome Light," sung at Vespers.
160. Services of Holy Week, Bridegroom Matins.
161. St. Gregory Nazianzus, *Dogmatic Poems*, PG 37.

ing to archaic intuition the springtime renewal is in some way an "anamnesis" or remembrance of the cosmic spring and of the original time in Paradise. "In order to remind us each year of the creation of the world God has made the spring in which all is in bud and in flower."[162] If spring is the moment of the world's creation, it must also be the moment of its re-creation, by virtue of the sacramentality of cosmic time, because God does nothing that is empty of meaning.

In order to purify time polluted by the sin of man, "Christ must rise from the dead at the precise instant of time at which sin entered."[163] There are three corresponding instants envisaged here, each heavy with the weight of its whole evolution in time: the instant of creation, in which contact with the eternal gives birth to the life of Paradise; the instant of the Fall, in which contact with the relativity of meonic non-being, toward which human freedom veers, admixes primitive time with being-unto-death and the stain of corruption is cast over human generations; and finally, the instant of the Resurrection, in which eternity rises up anew and from which transfigured time and duration proceeds, not simply to restore the time of Paradise but to transform fallen time into the vessel of eternity. There is a very close correspondence linking the two "sudden" instants, in which eternity first gives birth to and then resurrects time. "Because He had created a completely pure time in which man could take shape, and because this first time was stained by sin and was corrupted when man transgressed, despoiling the time to come, God took hold of the first times for the purpose of rectifying man, so that at the same time as he purified man, and by the very fact of purifying man from his passions, He also purified the age to come, even from its point of departure."[164] "Taking hold of the first times," that is, to give the cyclical return, the anniversary of the creation, the weight of a new beginning of creation itself, in the mysterious realism of the mimesis to which archaic forms of worship gave body.

---

162. Philo, *De Specialibus Legibus*.
163. *Pascal Homilies*, III, SC 48, Introduction.
164. *Pascal Homilies*, III, SC 48.

"In what season is Christ resurrected?" asks Cyril of Jerusalem. The Song of Solomon tells us: *"for lo the winter is past, the rain is over and gone. The flowers appear on the earth. The time of singing of birds is come."*[165] Now the earth is filled with flowers and the vines are being pruned. Because we are in April it is springtime. This is the time of the Jewish first month, the time of Passover: but then it was a symbolic Passover; now it is the real Pascha. This is the time of the creation of the world, for then it is that God said: *"Let the earth put forth vegetation, plants yielding seed and fruit trees bearing fruit in which is their seed, each according to its kind."*[166] And now, as you see, every plant is bearing seed. And just as God then created the sun and the moon and set them in the firmament to rule over the day and over the night, so, just a little while ago it was the time of the equinox. And God said, *"let us make man in our own image, after our likeness."*[167] Man has preserved the image of God but he has disfigured the likeness through his disobedience. Therefore in the same season that the Fall took place redemption was granted. In this season man was created, and disobeyed, and was expelled from Paradise. In the same season he obeyed by faith and returned to Paradise.

Salvation is granted in the same season as the Fall occurred, *"when the flowers appeared and it was the time of pruning the vines."*[168] Gregory of Nyssa, taking up the old symbolism that saw a return to the splendor of Paradise in the balance and luminous fullness of that moment at which the spring equinox and the full moon converge, showed how this was above all true in Christ's triumph: "the luminous life triumphs . . . the moon does not set without mixing its light with that of the sun, so that there is a single continuous light throughout the cycles of day and night,

165. Song of Solomon, 2:12 (RSV). Translator's note: Clément reads "le moment de la taille"—the time for pruning—for the time of singing.

166. Genesis 1:11

167. Genesis 1:26

168. St. Cyril of Jerusalem, *Catecheses*.

without a moment of darkness. May all your life be in the same manner a single feast and a glorious day, free from all darkness."[169]

When the Council of Nicea banned the celebration of Pascha on the 14th Nizan, it placed the primary emphasis on the opposite aspect of cyclical and lunar symbolism, what we have called repetition as a sign of hell. The moon was felt to be the queen of nocturnal terror and death, a diabolical Hecate. In fact, for the ancient Greeks and Hindus as for many primitive peoples, the moon was considered to be the abode of the dead, and the world under its power, subject to the endless cycles of the stars, was identified with the world of illusion and suffering. For Cyril of Alexandria, "the devil, prince of the night and of darkness," is symbolically called the moon and St. Augustine, commenting on Ecclesiastes, writes: "what fool changes like the moon if not Adam, in whom all have sinned? The human soul, distancing itself from sunlight and justice . . . has turned all its strength towards the external and becomes more and more darkened."[170] The luminous night of Pascha is symbolized by the lighting of candles. Taking place as the moon is waning, this symbolizes the "abolition of the moon," the victory of Christ over the devil, over evil, and over death. As Père Daniélou notes: "Christ's resurrection is at the same time the fulfillment of the cosmic feast of spring and of the feast of Passover. The Christian Easter takes on all of cosmic religion and Jewish religion."[171] Cyclical time is released from the despair that drove man to flee into the impersonal, and is henceforth inserted into the liturgy of the Living God, whose Incarnation has sanctified and made clear the meaning of each instant of cosmic time. Cyclical time is no longer rooted in nostalgia for the beginning: instead it is oriented, in an eschatological perspective, toward the expectation of the End, in which we are already participants in Christ. This is why St. Cyril of Jerusalem extends the parable of the seed, which must die in order to be reborn, to Christians, members of the Resurrected

---

169. *Letter 4*, PG 46.
170. PL 33
171. Dieu Vivant No. 18, *The Symbolism of Easter Day.*

One. The springtime renewal is a symbol of the resurrection of the dead: "these plants are dead in winter and green in springtime, and when the season comes they will be brought to life as if they have risen from the dead. Because God knows your lack of faith he has made the plants that you can see to be reborn each year: and so, observing what happens to inanimate life, you come to believe that this rebirth happens also for animate beings, endowed with life and reason."[172]

The Paschal week recapitulates the first week of creation and remakes the symbolism of the week, as "God took the whole of the time required for the creation in order to renew creation."[173] Sunday was chosen above all for the Resurrection, because it is the first day of the world, the day on which physical light was created, the symbol of the divine light that the Resurrection now gives to the world. "According to the original order of things, God made the light of the resurrection appear on the first day after the Sabbath, in accordance with the sequence of time. The first day of all time was once appointed as the beginning of physical light and now, by consequence, the first day is appointed as the beginning of the spiritual light of the resurrection."[174]

All the mystery of time and eternity is summed up in the meaning of the first day, the Lord's Day, as St. Basil showed.[175] Sunday is at one and the same time the first day and the eighth day, the beginning and the end, the moment at which eternity gives birth to time and the moment at which eternity welcomes in time. If the unfolding of the week symbolizes the unfolding of the whole universe, Sunday reveals God's design, conceived from the beginning of the world, "to unite all things in Christ."[176] Sunday is Paradise regained and the inauguration of life in the Resurrection, the miraculous suddenness of dawn, and the light without end of the eighth day, when God is finally all in all. Sunday draws

---

172. St. Cyril of Jerusalem, op. cit. p. 84.
173. Pascal Homilies, III, p. 136.
174. Ibid., p. 147.
175. St. Basil, *Homilies on the Hexameron*, SC 26.
176. Ephesians 1:10

together all the mystery of our salvation—it is the time created by Christ, recaptured by him and unfolding in him, in the Alpha and the Omega, the first, the last, the Living One.[177]

Christ has not only recapitulated all of human history, he has fulfilled it. As Oscar Cullmann pointed out, the final reality is presented in the person of the incarnate Word, whose greatness cannot be surpassed.[178] The Resurrection is the fulfillment of our time of waiting. Human nature, and through it the cosmos, is taken on by the hypostatic person of the Son of God and united by him to divine nature in a union of deification. The Ascension introduces human nature into the very heart of the Trinity. Everything is therefore fulfilled: the hypostatic union achieves the purpose for which the universe was created. The "fullness of time" opens the doors of the time of fullness. Henceforth Christ has passed from death to life in us. We are his human body becoming united to his transfigured, resurrected, and glorified Body through the "mysteries" of the Church. We sit with the Father "in the heavenly places in Christ Jesus."[179] God achieves his eternal plan of deification. "In these last times, the Word, having been united with the lowliness of our human nature, was made flesh by His love for mankind and, uniting himself to us, took on all of our human nature so that through the admixture of the divine, human nature would be deified with Him, all mortal clay being sanctified with these first fruits."[180] "Once and for all," as the Epistle to the Hebrews repeatedly hammers home, Christ entered "into the Holy Place . . . thus securing an eternal redemption [for us]."[181] Christ is the end of history.

History ends in Christ, yet history continues. For the fullness of being is offered to us and is not imposed. With Pentecost each person can, through the grace of the Holy Spirit, freely take part in the divine force that radiates from the glorified body of

---

177. Revelation 1:17
178. Cullmann, p. 75.
179. Ephesians 2:6 (RSV)
180. St. Gregory of Nyssa, *Adversus Apolinarem*, PG 45.
181. Hebrews 9:12-14 (RSV)

Christ. From now on history is the account of the fire that Christ has come to throw on the earth, that ceaselessly inflames the human soul, and of the light of the Holy Spirit, working on earth.

To conclude let us recall the argument so amply developed by Oscar Cullmann: if we can make sense of history, if history is to escape from the forces of cyclical repetition and destiny, if history is truly to be "our story," to be lived and not fled from, it is because of the unique feast of the Incarnation. This hammer blow is the foundation and the fulfillment of history. The Incarnation is not one event in a series, because all prior events only assume their full meaning in its light. This event "breaks the circles in which the impious wander,"[182] as St. Augustine so amply demonstrates in *The City of God*. God comes to us. To use St. Augustine's terms, this is an unheard of *novitas*, never repeated, *nulla repetita*, and allowing of no circular repetition, *nulla repetenda circuitu*. God comes to us to lead us to him. This is the straight path, the *via recta*, arising from the destruction of all false repetitions and cycles, *falsi circuli*. And this straight path, this history filled with infinitude, is none other than Christ.

It is true that sin continues its absurd repetition, suffocating our perception of the cosmic cycles with boredom. But these chains, this horizontal line made up of cycles welded together like so many links in a chain of slavery, this horizontal progression along a succession of the absurd, have been broken forever by the vertical event of the Incarnation. God became man, he descended even to death and to hell, and then ascended to the right hand of the Father, in order to unite even the most infernal temporal condition to divine eternity. He places us at the very heart of renewed time and lifts us out of the cycle of repetition and the captivity of sin, and allows us to encounter the Living God, and to slake our thirst with his own life, a life of such fullness that it cannot be other than eternal.

This encounter with the "Sun that never sets" introduces something new into human destiny, and by extension into the destiny of each person, that transforms their history. In meeting

---

182. Augustine of Hippo, *City of God*, Book 12.

the End of Time, time becomes history. In the final analysis, secular history and the history of revelation are one and the same. As, for better or worse, the gospel message reaches all nations on earth, humanity leaves cyclical time to enter into history, the history of revelation. From this moment, the time of torture and death becomes identified with that crucial moment on the cross, when suffering and death were swallowed up in glory. As the Body of the Crucified and Glorified Christ, the Church is the center of human time. Surpassing time, which it contains, the Church gives time its true value and makes it history.

Part Three

The Economy of the Holy Spirit and Deified Time

1.   The Double "Economy" of the Holy Spirit

The action of the Holy Spirit in the Church has two aspects that, from the moment of the Resurrection and of Pentecost, have given history its dimension of eternity. The Holy Spirit ensures the objective holiness of the Church as the Body of Christ: but it also opens to each person the path for their deification, according to the rules of the Spirit's own economy.

In the first instance, the Spirit unveils the presence of the Son in order to transmit by actualization the re-creation that is the work of the Son. In other words, the Spirit unceasingly presents to us, that is to say, makes us present to, the whole economy of the Son. "Remembering therefore what has been accomplished for us: the Cross, the Tomb, the Resurrection on the third day, the Ascension into Heaven and the Sitting at your Right Hand, and the Second and Glorious Coming Again," states the Liturgy of St. John Chrysostom. In the Liturgy, the faithful, who represent the Cherubim, are mystically united to one another, and Christ's glorified humanity is made apparent, in a small piece of matter transformed by the Spirit. Christ glorified is present at the right hand of the Father among the angels and is present to mankind in the Church, recapitulating all time, from the origins until its fulfillment.

The "remembering" at issue here is an ontologically realistic, rather than a psychological, event. The "ana-" in anamnesis marks the appearance, the return into consciousness, of a reality that was already secretly present. What is remembered is actualized, transforming the Christological event into current reality, into a Second Coming (Parousia) that arrives without ceasing. In Christ, eternity is united to time and the Spirit brings forth the time of the Savior, which is forever present in the eternal present in which his glorified humanity—his being-in time—dwells.

The time of the Church is communicated not through an undifferentiated eternity, but through time permeated with the eternity of the Savior. For the Church the ninth hour is every day identified with that ninth hour on which Christ was crucified, once and for all. A prayer at Nones (attributed to St. Basil) reads, "Lord and Master Jesus Christ, our God, you have led us to the present hour at which, hanging upon the cross, you prepared the way to Paradise for the thief and destroyed death by death." Likewise the events reported in the Gospels are not simply read and heard, but are seen in the Church. In this way, the Church is the eyewitness of the Lord, and for this reason the apostolic Church is wholly the witness and messenger of God.

As the Body of Christ, the Church makes Christ's eternity ever present through the action of the Holy Spirit. The Church is an extended sacrament in which the Spirit makes manifest the mystery of him who is the mystery that is manifested: Christ, the face of the Father. The most intimate reality of eternity, the mystery hidden in God before all time, is unveiled in the Church, to the angels' astonishment and for their instruction.[183] "The visible reality of the Lord and Redeemer has passed into the Sacraments," said St. Leo the Great,[184] and St. Ambrose wrote, "I see You who are invisible made visible in the Sacraments."[185] The presence of the glorified body of the Lord makes each sacrament a theophany, a transparent moment in which time reveals eternity. The

---

183. 1 Corinthians 2:7
184. PL 54, Sermon 74.
185. Apologia Proph. David, PL 14.

economy of the Son, made present by the action of the Spirit, fundamentally transforms the structure of time, from top to bottom. If Christ is the final moment already present, if the miracles of the Gospels are created anew by the Holy Spirit in the sacraments, then it is a mistake to consider the time of the Church as only another mode of linear time.[186] According to Chalcedonian teaching, sacramental time is time doubled with eternity, time transparent to eternity in the mysteries of the Church: it is in fact time deified. The sacramental moment places us within the glorified humanity of him in whom all that is to be unfolds, of him above all in whom the recapitulation of the unfolding present finds its eschatological fulfillment. In the incarnate Word, as we have said, all the antitypes of the Old Testament are found, the Word expressed in history, as well as the archaic theophanies, the cosmic expressions of the Word. Eschatology is fulfilled in him. Likewise, through the sacraments Christ "is and remains among us forever, in order to remain true to his promise."[187] For example, the water of baptism, flowing from the side of Christ, is the same water as that of the flood and of the Red Sea, those markers of sacred history. "Israel recaptured its freedom from Pharaoh by crossing the Red Sea: the world is granted freedom from sin by passing through the waters of baptism, according to the Word of God."[188] This water opens to us the two other "baptisms" of Blood—the Eucharist—and of Fire—the grace of Pentecost. The Church continues the freeing intervention of God, who led the Hebrews to cross the Red Sea, who led Christ through the waters of death, and who now, by means of the water in which one dies in order to be reborn, joins the body of the baptized to the Body of the Resurrected Christ. But the water of baptism is also the primordial water of Genesis: "the earth came from the waters and during the six days of creation the Spirit of God moved on the face of the waters. Water is the guiding force of the world."[189]

---

186. Cullmann
187. Cabasilas, *La Vie en Christ.*
188. St. Cyril of Jerusalem
189. St. Cyril of Jerusalem

This fertile water over which the Spirit moves is what all cosmic religions memorialize. They see water as the source of life, the sap and life force of the universe, the primordial substance, the tomb in which one dies through immersion, the womb from which one emerges renewed.[190] Finally, the baptismal water is the Kingdom in its limpid transfiguration, the sea of glass mixed with fire, on whose edge those who have conquered the Beast chant the Song of Moses, as sung triumphantly by the Israelites after crossing the Red Sea, and now joined for eternity to the Song of the Lamb.[191] "In the sacred laver of regeneration," writes St Cyril, "God has dried the tears on all the faces."[192]

Likewise the Eucharist, the true Passover, is the fulfillment of the messianic and nuptial promises that are linked in the Old Testament to the liturgical meal and, in particular, to the Passover feast. In sacred history, the manna and the living water of the Exodus prefigure the Eucharist, and are therefore recapitulated in the Eucharist. In the apocalyptic visions of the Old Testament, the inexhaustible nature of the messianic meal recalls the time of Paradise. In this way the Eucharist confirms the archaic intuition that the energies of God are present in the mystery of the earth and the seed. One cannot help but find an echo of the worship of Eleusis in the ode of the prefatory canon for communion: "most blessed earth, sanctified spouse of God, who made grow the unsown grain, the Saviour of the world." Finally, the Eucharist is above all eschatological: in the Eucharist the eon to come really comes to us; all is given; we touch the telos, the end point of all things. As *teleosis* the Eucharist is radiant with the glory that is to come. Gregory Palamas writes that certain saints saw light as an endless sea, flowing miraculously from a unique sun, that is to say, from the adored Body.[193]

The time of the Church is first and foremost a time of permanence, the time of the Incarnation, and still more, of Resur-

---

190. Eliade 2, ch. 5.
191. Revelation 15:1-3
192. St. Cyril of Jerusalem
193. St. Gregory Palamas, 3rd Triade.

rection and Ascension, by which the Lord lifts the created universe and all of nature within us and around us into the eternal light of the Trinity. Through the Church, therefore, present time includes *the ultimate moment*.[194] The Apocalypse shows us the crowd of the faithful here on earth taking part in the celestial liturgy.[195] If we call "history" only that part of human time that has been endowed with meaning, we can say not only that time has been endowed with meaning since the Incarnation, but that time encountered meaning, and that in God's turning toward his creation, absolute meaning came into the world and dwells here. From this moment there is a reality in the world that exceeds the world, opening a road leading beyond the world's diabolical autonomy. This reality is the Church, whose union of God and man places the earth on a continuum with heaven, and orients the march of mankind—whether toward or away from heaven. Heaven is already present in the eucharistic mystery of the Body of Christ. The proclamation of the word and the life of the Word made flesh make the Church itself an eschatological sacrament. It confronts the world and imposes a choice on the world. Eschatological time, the time of the Apocalypse, is the true historical time for mankind. The liturgical undertones of the Book of the Apocalypse have been often noted, particularly John's description of the Church in the terms of the Jewish liturgy, as temple and molten sea.[196] The Temple is both of the world and beyond the world. As the body of the Resurrected, "heaven on earth," the Church is more than just another subject for sociological analysis. Christians are deeply mistaken if they only come together collectively to oppose other earthly collective bodies. The Church exists in the world as an opening, an exorcism: it is a mortal wound for this idolatrous and deceitful world, but for the created world it is the offer of transfiguration: "Where the carcass is, there will the eagles be gathered."[197]

194. Translator's note: italics in original.
195. Revelation 7:9
196. 1 Kings chapter 7
197. Matthew 24:28

Christ took on our nature in order to renew it. But the individual person is not taken: a person gives of himself. Here the economy of the Holy Spirit and the grace of Pentecost come into play. Through the sacrament of chrismation, whose illuminating power is a renewed Pentecost, the Spirit grants each of us, *from within*,[198] the possibility of assuming a new life, and of "enhypostasizing" a renewed human nature through personal sanctification, as revealed by the sacraments. The holy power (*dynamis hagiastikè*) enables each Christian to bring the divine adoption to fruition in his own way, thus becoming a "co-heir" of Christ. The economy of the Holy Spirit thus makes Christ not only the true Adam but also the first-born, the "first fruits" and the "beginning" of the new creation.[199] Christian life is not only integration into the Body of Christ but also the personal encounter of each Christian with Christ, in the irreducible diversity of each person's hypostasis, touched by the Holy Spirit. In the humanity of the incarnate Word, everything is given or rather, everything is offered. Everything must be freely lived in the Spirit for the person, becoming one body with his Lord, to be able to meet him in the nuptial wonder of the Song of Solomon. "The love of Christ in the Holy Spirit is in fact the knowledge of God."[200] By means of the unending grace of Pentecost a multiplicity of persons each in their own way "filled with the Spirit" lend their force to the unity of the Church.[201] The relationship between the economy of the Son and the economy of the Holy Spirit is one of mutual service and reciprocity, rather than a one-sided dependence. This is the earthly reflection of the mystery of the Trinity. In the West this has been partially warped by the shift in emphasis of the "filioque." The Father is the sole source of divinity and the Spirit cannot originate from the Person of the Son, without confounding unity and diversity and implying the destruction of the "monar-

---

198. Translator's note: italics in original.
199. Colossians 1:15-18; 1 Corinthians 15:20
200. Origen, PG 17.
201. Ephesians 5:18

chy"[202] of the Father. But the begetting of the Son and the procession of the Spirit cannot be comprehended one without the other: one cannot separate out a dyad from the Trinity.[203] The setting up of opposites, that product of our fallen state, is always overcome by the mystery of the Trinity. The begetting of the Son and the procession of the Spirit are ontologically simultaneous. The Son is begotten "at the same time" that the Spirit proceeds. The Spirit proceeds "at the same time" that the Son is begotten. This is the eternal source of the reciprocity that joins the Son and the Spirit in a single economy, "these two hands of the Father," in the words of St. Irenaeus. As we have seen, the Spirit witnesses to the Son and the action of the Spirit gives order to the act of redemption that is made present. To make the Spirit an attribute of Christ would take away the hypostatic character of the Spirit, so clearly emphasized by Christ when he spoke of "another comforter."[204] If the Spirit was an attribute of Christ, the time of the Church would be a divine comedy enacted by God alone, in which Christ takes hold of men and women (or at least some of them) in order to swallow them up in his unity. Under this conception, man can do nothing and history is no more. The crucial point is that the Spirit is not only a means but an end: *Christ came for the Spirit, to make possible the fullness of the descent of the Spirit, to mold the vessel of Pentecost.*[205] The whole goal of Christ's work of salvation is that believers receive the Holy Spirit, and that the Spirit becomes, as it were, the soul of our soul, so that we are sanctified and regenerated in intelligence, conscience, and in all our feelings, by the energy of the Holy Spirit.[206] In this sense, the economy of the Son gives order to the economy of the Spirit. The Church is only

---

202. Monarchy: *monè arché*, the sole principle, the unique origin
203. Father-Son, Father-Spirit, or, as implied by the filioque, (Father-Son) – Spirit.
204. In the same passage St. John refers to the Spirit as "he" and not as "it." In Acts, the Spirit speaks personally on many occasions: for example, "the Spirit said to Philip." There is a tendency to confuse the Spirit, the third Person of the Trinity, which descended on Christ and which descends on the Church, with the *nous Christou*, the mind of Christ.
205. Translator's note: italics in original.
206. St. Simeon, the New Theologian

the Body of Christ in order to be the place in which humans are sanctified, "deified," and receive the Holy Spirit. Certainly, each person should, like Christ, unite in himself the human and the divine—human nature and the divine energy that the Spirit communicates. By the anointing of the Spirit, each person becomes a "christ": "the anointing which you have received from Him abides in you . . . and the same anointing teaches you concerning all things, and is true."[207] Indeed, this union of the created and the uncreated is accomplished here in a created being, by grace as the communication of divine life. What is consecrated is nothing less than the uniqueness of the person: this is so fundamental that it cannot be subsumed into part of the whole, whether that be the Church or another person, not even the person of Christ. The unique person takes on the totality of the Church, and must become the Body of Christ through the contemplation of his face and through communion with all other persons. This communion in which individual conscience becomes personal conscience is catholicity—that is to say, an opening to Spirit-Tradition in the lived unity of the Body of Christ.

Thus the Christian finds himself in a threefold position: "vertically," in communion with God, that permits and demands communion with one's neighbor, and "horizontally," in the diverse array of humanity crowned by the flames of the Spirit, coming into the unity of human nature as recapitulated and glorified by Christ. This is a threefold position because in the Trinity each Person is not merely a part of the divine: each Person expresses the divine nature in a unique manner, or, rather, is a unique communication of the divine gift, because oneness is total abandon, or communion. To restate St. John's definition, the Church is a *koinonia* and its goal is the deification of the human person in the grace of the Holy Spirit. The never-ending day of Pentecost makes each Christian a *personal* witness to the truth, a co-worker, *synergos, aware* of God.[208] And since each person is, by definition, free—free not just to choose "to be saved" but to accept or refuse

---

207. 1 John 2:27
208. See 1 Corinthians 3:9 (translator's note: italics in original).

the new life that God offers—history becomes no longer a pious puppet show but instead the scene of deadly serious encounters and courtship battles.

History becomes the embrace of personal lives, of the drama of men and women who, "having ears that hear," listen and bear fruit. Each baptism, each conversion in which baptismal grace is made present, confirms the encounter of two loves, that of God and that of man. A person who is open to the Spirit becomes ever more conscious of this encounter, in an existential consciousness that engages the whole being. If, in the old tradition, the Orthodox faithful congratulate and embrace those who have just taken communion, it is because they understand that an event of such importance in time and eternity has just transpired between this person and God, that it eclipses even the most irreducible "facts" of worldly history, or rather, that it alone can fully elucidate their meaning.

The time of the Church is the time of the Spirit making its way into the innermost secrets of the heart. Time is the patience of God, measuring out for humanity the manifestation of his love, so that, when the fire of this love is completely unveiled, it is a fire that heals and not a fire that consumes. God "is not slow with his promise . . . but he is patient with you, because he does not want any to be destroyed, but all to come to repentance."[209] As the Fathers so often pointed out, history leads to the realization of the fullness of deified humanity. This is the expectation of the martyrs and of God himself. Our history is determined as we choose for or against Christ, in the depths of our humility that opens to us the breath of the Spirit, in the synergy of grace and our love, a synergy that grants power to our royal priesthood, to exorcise, to intercede, and to transfigure. In this way we become co-workers in the final abolition of death and in the cosmic transfiguration, co-workers whose saintly way of life, in the words of the Apostle, urges on the coming of the day of God.[210] "And another angel came and stood at the altar holding a golden censer, and

---

209. 2 Peter 3:9
210. 2 Peter 3:11

there was given to him much incense, for him to place it with the prayers of all the saints in the golden censer which is before the throne. And the smoke went up from the incense, by the prayers of the saints, from the hand of the angel before God. And the angel took the censer and filled it with fire from the altar and cast it upon the earth, and there came thunders and voices and lightnings and earthquake."[211] The prayers of the saints, united to the altar service of the angels, bring closer the apocalyptic fire that we know to be at once death and resurrection.

The time of the Church therefore culminates when every person is aware that the End is already present and that history (in Christ) has already been consummated. The Parousia, the Second Coming, signifies not only coming but expectation, and not only expectation but presence. To borrow an expression from St. Seraphim of Sarov, the time of the Church is the time of the "acquisition of the Holy Spirit."[212]

There are therefore three major aspects that characterize the period stretching from the First to the Second Coming of the Lord: the tension between time and eternity, the eschatological character of time itself, and the construction of the Kingdom of God.

---

211. Revelation 8:2-5
212. This is a matter of existential knowledge communicated to the whole being and to its social world and cosmic environment, and not simply a matter of intellectual knowledge. Fedorov, in particular, demonstrated that the separation of knowledge and life is itself the very mark of sin.

2.   The Tension between Time and Eternity: Apocalypse and *Kenosis* of the Holy Spirit

The ancient era is still present with us, the new era is not yet fully apparent, and the tension between the two cannot always be resolved in human history. We still live in the fallen world; we cry out "Come, O Lord"[213]; we wait for the time at which the last enemy, death, will be conquered,[214] when God will incontestably be all in all.[215] "Dear friends, we are God's children now; what we shall be has not yet been revealed."[216] The Fathers make it clear that the age of evangelization in which we live is only the shadow of our participation in the age to come, in the celestial Jerusalem in which the heart of all mysteries will be revealed. "For now we see by a mirror, obscurely, but then face to face."[217]

Origen describes the third Passover, the third Pascha, the Pascha of eternity, which will clearly reveal everything to us concerning the Son of God, just as he is fully unveiled in heaven.[218] St. Ambrose called the Old Testament "the shadow," the New Testament "the image," and the Kingdom itself "the truth." We should note that he charges the word "image" with meaning.[219] St. Gregory Palamas states that the hidden depths of dogma are to be revealed in time to come.[220] Vladimir Lossky states that "the age of the Old Testament lived by faith and steered towards hope, while the age of the Gospel lives in hope and steers towards love: and that love is a mystery that will not be revealed and will not be fully achieved until the time to come."[221]

However, you only have to read St. John the Evangelist to know that life has definitively triumphed: "the life was re-

---

213. Revelation 22:20
214. 1 Corinthians 15:26
215. 1 Corinthians 15:28
216. 1 John 3:2
217. 1 Corinthians 13:12
218. Origen, *Commentary on St. John*, PG 14.
219. St. Ambrose, *Commentary on Psalm 38*.
220. *Tome Hagioritique*, PG 150.
221. Lossky

vealed"[222]; "he who listens to my words and believes in Him who sent me has life everlasting."[223] To live according to love is to be in the light, because "the darkness is passing away and the true light is now shining."[224]

History shows us that the tension is irreducible. The Church is in the world not just as a proclamation but as the present realization of the Kingdom, and yet the Church is not of this world. The entire universe is summoned to enter into the Church and be transfigured: and yet God will not be all in all until the end of time. "The King, the Lord Jesus, has come, and his kingdom is to come."[225] History will continue to be an apocalyptic battle until the Second Coming.

It is true that Soloviev, systematizing Russian religious philosophy's nostalgia for oneness, held onto the dream of a perfect theocracy, of a state based on organized love, fulfilling the ideal of the perfect Good here on earth, and reconciling God and Caesar—the emperor, the pope, and the inspired philosopher. However, in his last work, *The Tale of the Antichrist*, he points out that this perfect order, set up by "a great spiritual master" for the greatest happiness of soul and body, could only belong to the Antichrist[226]. The coming of the Kingdom will not be accomplished in history but only in its dislocation and its transfiguration, through the happy catastrophe of the Parousia.

As for Fedorov's grand design, in which science and human technology are internalized through ascetic effort, in order to resurrect our ancestors here on earth, so that they may even now take part in the blessings with which progress has mastered the planet—if this would recall half-asleep Christians to their duty to struggle for the definitive triumph of life, it would also tame this struggle by disassociating it from the Parousia. This leads Fedorov's contemporary disciples to ridicule the cross,

222. 1 John 1:2
223. John 5:24
224. 1 John 2:8
225. G. Florovsky, *Le Corps du Christ Vivant*, in La Sainte Eglise Universelle, Paris-Neuchâtel, 1948, p. 67.
226. V. Soloviev, *Three Conversations* (1900).

which they denounce as the banner of death—that same cross that destroyed death.

To resurrect the Fathers, to establish a perfect natural order on earth—does this not require that all men become believers and that Christians become the political elite of humanity? But "the servant is not greater than his master" and Christ promised us nothing but persecution on earth. "If he is the King of Israel, let him come down from the cross and we will believe in him."[227] When we hear this challenge, and even more the silence that answers it (may God grant us that silence) we begin to understand why, as we said earlier, fullness is offered but not imposed, and why, therefore, God has permitted the time of sin and death. The duality that is the Kingdom and the world guarantees free space to each of us, rather than our submission as a charmed animal. It is true that "God became man so that man can become god." But what else could the Pantocrator do than declare his love to man and ask only that man repay him in kind?[228]

Is not the apex of divine humility seen in the survival of the fallen world, the world in which man can believe in his own autonomy? Is this not the supreme mark of God's respect for our freedom? The manifestation of glory is restrained by divine economy, for otherwise where would be the space for personal dignity, human trials, and collaboration? Graham Greene illustrates the discretion and humility of divine love in writing, for example, that the Eucharist "places God at the mercy of men who barely understand the meaning of mercy."[229] He here intuitively reformulates an old dogma, albeit inexactly. Inexactly, that is, from an Orthodox viewpoint, in which the time of the Church, the time after Christ's Resurrection and Ascension, cannot be defined as the continuation of Christ's self-abnegation and humiliation, of Christ's *kenosis*. What are the Church and the Eucharist if not the offering of Christ's *glorified* Body to mankind? Beyond the humble bread and wine God remains infinitely awesome: the Or-

---

227. Matthew 27:42
228. N. Cabasilas, op. cit. p. 53.
229. Graham Greene, *The Heart of the Matter*, 1954.

thodox approach communion with fear and trembling, knowing that it is a fire that burns at the same time that it purifies, a fire that purifies through burning. "He who eats the loaf or drinks the cup unworthily is guilty against the Blood and Body of the Lord . . . For anyone who eats and drinks is eating and drinking his own damnation if he does not recognize the Body. For that reason many among you are weak and sick, and a good many have even died."[230] The Eucharist is not an instrument of human will and God is not at man's disposition. There can be no "change" without the union of two wills, divine and human, without the faith and prayer of the faithful, that is to say without the epiclesis—that meeting of human freedom and the grace of the Holy Spirit.

Nevertheless, who can deny continued divine humility and *kenosis*, when the God of love holds back the intensity of his love, when God cannot give himself and reveal himself fully, when God must wait to manifest his presence in glory, because to man in his state of refusal and hatred, this revelation would appear as hellfire. This *kenosis* is no longer that of the Son, who now sits in glory: it is the effacement, the anonymity—one might even say the non-revelation—of the Holy Spirit. For we owe everything to the Spirit: through the Spirit we are guided to confess the divinity of Jesus and to call on God as Father. Yet we cannot name the Spirit himself. God is holy all-in-all; God is Spirit all-in-all. By these words the gift that we receive from the Spirit is communicated, without shedding light on the Spirit that is the giver. Still more, the living water of the Gospel and the fire of Pentecost communicate to us the inflowing of divine life, but are silent on the mysterious third Person of the Trinity that makes this life well up in the very core of our being. The *kenosis* of the Spirit is thus the inverse of that of the Son. Tortured, cursed, and hung upon the cross, Jesus appeared incontestably human: his divine nature was hidden completely in the "form of a servant." The descent of the Holy Spirit, on the other hand, manifests divinity, but its dazzling impact masks the personal character of the Spirit who communicates the divine. In giving, the Spirit adapts the gift to our own singularity and to our

---

230. 1 Corinthians 11:29-30

weakness, with a humility and delicacy that permits each of us to discover the personal impact of grace.

It is through the Holy Spirit that the Trinity "breaks down" the wall of transcendence and is eternally made manifest in glory, because divine energy has its source in the Father, and is brought to us by the Son in the Holy Spirit. And so, in this convulsion, this luminous "lightning-stroke" through which the "closed" Trinity of absolute transcendence becomes the "open" Trinity of glorious revelation, the Spirit, the third Person of the Trinity, remains hidden, to ensure that the fullness of the divine flames forth. And in this way the Spirit, the third Person of the Trinity, mysteriously fully one with transfigured Glory, is at the same time wholly identified with the *economia*, the rolling out of God's will on earth, of which the goal is to make created beings participants in this glory. That is to say, the Spirit is mysteriously identified with the kenosis of the divine, which, through respect for our personal dignity, allows the continuation of the time of death, of the eon enslaved to the "prince of this world," even after the definitive victory of Christ over the devil and over death.

The Son bears witness to the Father. The Spirit bears witness to the Son. But who will bear witness to the Spirit if not the translucent saints? The Spirit will only be fully revealed in the Kingdom, in the *pleroma* of deified humanity, and these illumined human beings will bear witness to the Spirit. But history has already sketched out this revelation in the communion of the saints throughout the ages, which St. Simeon the New Theologian called the "gold chain" of sainthood. "The saints joined and united by the Spirit . . . come from generation to generation . . . joining themselves to those who came before and being illumined, like them, by their participation in the grace of God. They become like a golden chain, each one a link joined in faith to his predecessor, joined in works and in charity, until in the One God they form a chain that cannot easily be broken."[231] In this succession the past is not abolished, because the saints participate in Christ's victory over death. The saint receives only in order to give. The

---

231. *Chapitres Théologiques*, SC 51.

souls of the saints, awaiting resurrection in the spiritual heaven, enter with the angels into this chain of illumination and participate in the gift of the Holy Spirit. In the Church's uniting of God and man, the light descending from heaven to earth is refracted in a rainbow of transfigured faces, the icons that fill our churches, that encompass us in "the cloud of witnesses." Translucent members of the glorified Body of Christ, manifold hypostases of divine energy, they write the name of the Unnameable in letters of fire and in spiritual constellations, and the Unnameable himself is inexhaustibly revealed in each trait of their personhood, in each unique feature that becomes transparent, in the torrent of newness, that is to say, in the best offerings of time.

But in opposition to the newness of the person that reveals the Holy Spirit, we find individual and collective repetition and the opacity of sin, which conceal the Spirit. Having placed a crown of thorns on Christ, humanity masks the adored presence of the Unnameable with its own cloak of self-sufficiency and despair.

The revelation of the Spirit is the holy of holy of the Church. If we lose sight of the full personal worth of the Spirit, either by changing the Spirit's reciprocal relationship with the Son into one of dependence (as does the *filioque*) or by opposing the Spirit to the objectivity of the Son's Body (as do the illuminists) we enclose the Spirit within his own *kenosis*, making the Spirit a simple function either of the Son, or of the inspired individual. Let us remember Christ's terrible warning: will not humanity's response to the Holy Spirit be the key to the history of Christianity, the key to all history since Pentecost?

The *kenosis* of the Spirit is also the *kenosis* of the Church. You have to look closely to see the real beauty of the face of the Church, a face that is forever stained by our sins.[232] We are all familiar with the debatable aspects of the theory of the "Third Rome," promulgated in Russia in the fifteenth and sixteenth centuries. But certain popular versions of this theory contain elements that are instructive as to the *kenosis* of the Church. The legend of the "Capuchon Blanc" (white hood) tells us that Emper-

---

232. Origen, *In Cant. Canticorum, Com. 4.*

or Constantine, having been healed and converted by Pope Sylvester, wanted to give him a royal crown as a sign of gratitude. But an angel commanded him to give a crown, not of earthly power but of heavenly witness, in the form of the Capuchon Blanc, the symbol of Christ's Resurrection on the third day.[233]

The Capuchon Blanc stayed in Rome until the day that the papacy, succumbing to the "Latin heresy," proclaimed the earthly dominion of the Church. At that time the angel commanded that the Capuchon Blanc be sent to Constantinople. But soon the "Second Rome" was threatened by infidels and the patriarch, warned in a dream by Constantine and Sylvester, had the relics transported to Russian soil, to Novgorod. "For," said Pope Sylvester to the patriarch, "the old Rome has strayed from the Christian faith through its pride and its desire for power, that have led it into the Latin heresy. And in the new Rome faith will also perish from the violence of the infidels. It is in the Third Rome, on Russian soil, that the grace of the Holy Spirit will shine."

Does this not encapsulate the image of the wandering Church, of the woman of the Apocalypse defending from the dragon the child that she will bring into the world? "Flung down upon the earth, the dragon pursued the woman."[234] The devil was mortally wounded by Christ's Resurrection, a spiritual battle in which the destiny of creation itself was at stake. The devil lies on the earth in agony and in earthly time, and Christians must wrestle "not against flesh and blood, but . . . against the spirits of evil in heaven"[235] who have been "uprooted" by the cross. "There were given to the woman the two wings of the great eagle, so that she might fly into the desert."[236] The Church is preserved and guided in its wanderings by the power of the Holy Spirit. The Church does not have a fixed place. She finds refuge, now here, now there, and the Spirit transforms persecution, the normal historical condition of the Church, into "desert": the spiritual state of penitence

---

233. The name of this legend indicates its roots in monastic spirituality.
234. Revelation 12:13
235. Ephesians 6:12
236. Revelation 12:14

and prayer, in which Christians look to God for everything and are fed by the manna of the Eucharist.

"See, I stand at the door and knock."[237] This God, rejected by his creation, by the perversion of freedom by fallen angels and sinful humanity, this is the mystery of kenosis. Nevertheless we should not forget the other aspect of Providence: God is "outside" (from the viewpoint of those displaced intellects whose sinful vision engenders the bad externality of the world) but he is not inactive. He knocks at the door of the cosmos, of history, of the human body and soul. *He acts on anthropo-cosmic nature in order to awaken and warn humanity.*[238] The Book of Revelation describes in symbolic terms this critical aspect of the tension between time and eternity, between the fallen eon and the God who has come and will come again. We cannot exhaustively interpret these symbols, because their reality will only be fully revealed in the Kingdom and they must remain, even for the saints who share the ways of God, more an existential than a descriptive reality. This is why the Book of Revelation is not some kind of historical narrative that we must make correspond, episode by episode, to history unfolding on earth. The Book of Revelation is, in its totality, a "screen" by means of which we can discern the full spiritual meaning of *every* historical event, as the confrontation of man and God lays bare not only the earthly cosmos but also the invisible universes of demons and angels.

In purely schematic terms, one could say that the Book of Revelation brings us into the presence of two forms of temporal existence. The one is "heavenly," a time deified with splendor and adoration that blossoms in the world, both from on high, through the splendor of the cosmos, and through the liturgy and the sanctity of each person encountered—in short in the Church as the heart of the cosmic liturgy. The whole universe joins in the heavenly liturgy through the rhythm of the liturgy on earth. "And I looked, and I heard the voice of many angels in a circle about the throne and the animals and the elders, and the number of

237. Revelation 3:20
238. Translator's note: italics in original.

them was myriads of myriads and thousands of thousands, saying in a great voice: The Lamb who has been sacrificed is worthy to receive the power and the glory and the wisdom and the strength and the honor and the glory and the blessing. And I heard all creation, whatever is in the sky and on the earth and beneath the earth and in the sea, and everything which is within these, I heard them saying: To him who sits upon the throne and to the Lamb, blessing and honor and glory and power forever and ever. And the four animals said: Amen; and the elders fell down and worshiped."[239]

At the heart of deified time God wipes the tears of "those who come from the great suffering." On its borders the Christian people carry out their royal ministry, working with the harvesting angels so that all people may be saved.[240] "Because You alone are holy, because all the nations will come and worship before You, because Your judgments are made manifest."[241] This "heavenly" time, one might say, is the divine *economia* seen from the inside, as seen by those who give themselves over without reserve, setting forth on a road that leads to the vast love of God the Three in One, or dare we say, of God contemplated from "within."

Opposed to this, there is terrestrial time or rather demoniacal time, that of the divine *economia* viewed from without, the shards of its terrible collision with a blasphemous and idolatrous humanity that allows itself to be enslaved by the "prince of this world," by the "god of this fallen eon." In an apparent paradox, the Incarnation, this revelation of love, has greatly amplified the thunder strikes of divine "rage" against "the idolaters and all who love and do falsehood."[242] From the moment of the Incarnation, transcendence is immanent within time itself and strikes the human heart at the deepest roots of a person's non-being, so that he can no longer seek refuge apart from Christ. In Christ the distance between the created and the uncreated is eliminated, the

---

239. Revelation 5:11-14
240. 1 Timothy 2:4
241. Revelation 15:4
242. Revelation 22:15

hell of our fallen condition is illuminated, and the void opens up and is filled with light. If God comes to us in every situation, under every reality of our fallen condition—even the most awful—if God comes first to the assassins and the prostitutes, a person's only resort, if they wish to continue in flight and refusal, is their personal freedom. If the divine light reaches to the very depths of darkness, a person cannot shut out that light except in their own being, in that darkness that they themselves create: and even then, if they turn aside and plunge into the heart of their non-being, they will discover the Crucified One. In the very depths, they will encounter forgiveness. Only by continuing to blaspheme and to judge themselves can they maintain the darkness. Eternity acts on time from the inside. It is no longer "out there." Death has been conquered. Each person must now make a rigorous choice. Divine love surrounds them and everything for them depends on that *metanoia*, that turning around in the spiritual core of one's whole being, that tears a person away from the shadows of the self-worshiping "I" and opens them to the grace of the Holy Spirit. In that moment Satan is already mortally wounded and vanquished. If Satan is permitted by God to strike at mankind it is in order to summon mankind to repentance. In fact it is God who chastises those he loves, so that the zeal for repentance will burn in their hearts. Confronted through Providence with the greatest of love, a person either feels the grain of holiness begin to catch fire within, a glowing coal that will sooner or later flame with the breath of the Holy Spirit; or they close themselves up in their darkness, as they are ceaselessly dissolved by the "unfolding light" and enter into a mere "secondary" existence (like the "second death" of which the Book of Revelation speaks). This is an existence without true reality, of choice alone, in which you pound on your eyes with your fists in order to extinguish the sun.

All the cataclysms of history and the cosmos flow from this refusal, because man lives with man, and man is responsible for the universe. God restricts himself to turning these inevitable cataclysms to the good. He knocks at the door of sinful humanity. The day of judgment, like the mystery of the cross, forms part of history. And the cross, to use one of the powerful images of early Christianity, has two aspects, one of light and one of darkness. On the one side, the resurrected Christ in his glory. On the other side, Satan in agony until the end of the world. Through the Apocalypse, the way of the cross of human history, humanity must move from judgment, in which Satan and all his followers are crucified, to the "judgment of judgments" that opens into love and transfiguration.

This is why, contrary to the spirit of accommodation to the myths of our time pursued by too many Christians, the time of the Church is neither evolution nor progress but instead a choice out of the catastrophe, a *prise de conscience*, the act of awareness of the "crisis" (a word which in its fullest sense designates judgment).

What crisis? First of all, historical crises, the "white horseman" of pride and lust for power followed by war on his "flaming red horse" and by death on his "pallid green horse." In other words, man turns his non-being into an absolute, and from this act those souls deprived of the Word of God and of the bread of life devour each other and are therefore condemned to spiritual death. All political drama is only a commentary in unfolding history on the personal drama of sinful humanity.

Secondly, cosmic crises, insofar as humanity, instead of sanctifying nature by offering it to God, sucks away its lifeblood in order to become equal with the gods. Nature itself rebels in face of the rebel. Having been blind for so long to its "cosmic responsibility," the modern world has suddenly and brutally discovered the consequences of its depredation, whether soil erosion, air pollution, or nuclear contamination. The plagues described in the Apocalypse reveal the true meaning of our plundering of the planet and of the disintegration of matter. But the reality is even more mysterious. The earthly cosmos does not stand alone in the vastness of creation: it is surrounded by invisible universes, some angelic, some demonic. According to many of the Fathers, the order and majesty of the world is under the guard of the angels and is illuminated with their radiance. The angels are the servants of the divine energy that penetrates and animates all things. Their presence is to some extent the acme, the *entelekhia*, the perfection of created organisms, the invisible form that shapes all growth and sets the rhythm of unfolding creation.

Now, according to St. Paul, there are rival angels that are the usurpers of the cosmos, who through their spells are the servants of the "father of all lies." They attempt to subjugate nature and to pervert its beauty so as to enchant mankind. The lives of the saints show how the demons employ the elements to disturb the prayers of the hermits. A person's actions have the power either to exorcise our universe and unite it to the choir of angels, or to deliver it into the depths of hell, according to whether they are aligned with or opposed to grace. A person can become a "fount of the abyss" spreading a black smoke of lies and illusion, a darkness that renders human vision ever more opaque to the divine glory that the angels come to announce.

Both historical and cosmic crises result in the degradation and the further corruption of humanity. Mankind falls prey to those sicknesses of the soul that are still scarcely understood by our contemporary medicine. To take a simplistic example, in the sixteenth century cancer was held to arise from the "black bile of melancholy." Now we know that it is a monstrous proliferation of hostile cells that attack the organism itself. Is there not a clear parallel here to the condition of man separated from God and from his neighbor? Is this not the prototype for the disease of atheism? "And there was a sad sore wound inflicted upon the men who have the mark of the Beast and worship his image."[243] But here also we must go deeper. We are moved only by physical suffering. But imagine for a moment an angel hurrying through the well-fed towns and cities of the West. Will not the angel be as shocked by the ulcerous state of our souls, as we are by the sight of bodies ravaged by famine? And just as the starving gnaw on dirt and leaves before dying, so unassuaged spiritual hunger drives the soul to gorge on the poisons of the Beast. Have you never been struck by those empty faces, divorced from reality, by those facial masks, by the discontinuity of the mask borne in the present moment, by this death of the human face that seems

---

243. Revelation 16:2

to characterize our age of happiness? We no longer know how to read the Book of Revelation, as we lack the most elementary tools of spiritual discernment. We treat history as we treat the faces that surround us—as a superficial gloss. In its unseen depths, in the ultimate reality of lives that open into the unseen, history becomes the Apocalypse. In this secret space, eternity enters into and transfigures earthly time, uniting it to the heavenly liturgy, or on the contrary, jettisoning it into the darkness of freedoms gone wild, into the mortal combat in which Christ's victory is made real. Such is the apocalyptic battle between St. Michael and the dragon. Michael's name itself, "who is like God?" is a condemnation of all idolatry, especially of the collective and individual self-idolatry of man: "You will be like God, knowing good and evil," whispered the serpent.[244] The guardian angel of the Old Testament Temple, Michael takes on the same role for the Christian Church.

According to Jewish tradition, he offers "lambs of fire"—that is to say, the souls of the righteous—on the altar on high. Michael's battle with the dragon pulses through the history of the Church. The dragon feeds the persecution that destroys bodies, and the seduction that destroys souls, whereas St. Michael triumphs with the martyrs. Visible history in its unfolding is none other than the materialization of this confrontation taking place in that interior and objective heaven onto which the human "heart" opens.

On the one hand, we are faced with a growing "dehumanization," which, if such a neologism may be permitted, results in a corresponding "decosmification," to the extent that, in the final convulsions, even the regularity of cosmic rhythms will collapse and the sun will darken and will become the devourer of life, instead of the life giver.[245] The time of idolatry and blasphemy will collapse under the thrust of eternity. And just as many have become ill because they have taken communion "without acknowledging" the presence of Christ in all faith and in all humility, so

244. Genesis 3:5
245. Matthew 24:29-30; Revelation 15:8-9

too "the world" has become ill by harboring this wound of eternity, the Church-as-Eucharist, without recognizing it. A person only reaches full personhood in going beyond themselves into the communion of love that created them and that wills to recreate them. *The person who rejects God becomes as one possessed.* There is no middle ground. This is the apocalyptic truth ignored by a certain kind of optimistic Christianity, that imagines the "infidels" "sailing unknowingly on the waters of sanctifying grace and maintaining an inalienable charity even in the midst of the most evident depravity."[246] Nothing and no one can remain neutral: and all is ambiguous; everything is part of the battleground. It is true that many sleepwalk as if possessed: "Father, forgive them, for they know not what they do."[247] But he who spoke this prayer was crucified by the sleepwalkers, and the Christian should expect no less from the mediocrity of daily life.

On the other hand, the Gospel is proclaimed and the martyrs bear witness. For the believer, history contracts vertiginously, becoming the time of trial between the two comings of the Savior. "Simon, Simon, behold, Satan asked for you, to sift you like grain, but I asked for you that your faith should not fail you."[248] In the soul of the faithful, every catastrophe resounds as a summons to greater humility and to greater love, and thus to a more naked witness. This will reveal to the world that from henceforth the mystery of death, the death of one and the death of all, announced in the "crises" of history and the convulsions of the natural world, is now the "mystery" of the cross, that is to say, the Resurrection. We must bear witness to the light even in the heart of the darkness that does not wish to receive the light, as the time is short, as the darkness cannot prevail over the light. The light will illumine everything and our prayer arises to implore, and perhaps to ensure, that this may be the light of transfiguration and not the consuming fire.

---

246. L. Bouyer, preface to L. Casserly, *Absence du Christianisme*, 1957.
247. Luke 23:34
248. Luke 22:31-32

From one direction comes the Antichrist and from the other comes Christ. This is not due to some so-called equality or polarity. That cannot be, for one is the fullness of being and the other is a nothingness that sucks out being, exploiting the freedom of the created being. But Christ permits the Antichrist, so that the choice should be ineluctable. One should not doubt the reality of the Antichrist. But his name is also a "cipher" that reveals a certain dimension of history to believers, the actions of innumerable "antichrists" whose history the Antichrist recapitulates.[249] "You have heard that the Antichrist is coming, even so there are now many antichrists."[250] The Antichrist is the perversion of political power become absolutism; it is the first beast of the Apocalypse; it is the pseudo-religion of the false prophet. "For false Christs will rise up and false prophets, and they will present great signs and portents, so as to mislead even the chosen, if that may be done."[251] The Antichrist not only denies "that Jesus is the Christ"[252] but he also mimics Christ in a parody of the Resurrection: "and one of his heads (that of the beast of the sea) was as if stricken to death, and his death blow had been healed. Then the whole world went in wonder after the Beast."[253] As for the beast of the sea (in Jewish apocalyptic literature the "earth" and the "sea" symbolize Israel and the Gentiles), "he makes great portents [a parody of Pentecost], so that he even makes fire come down from the sky to earth in the sight of man."[254]

After the twentieth century, the Christian knows the brutal urgency of this immense effort to organize life not only apart from Christ but in fact against Christ, denouncing him as the enemy of life, and offering man not only bread but also ecstasy. The temptation of the modern world, wrote Paul Claudel, lies in showing that we have no need of God in order to do good. In fact, it is claimed that the human condition can be remedied by

---

249. St. Irenaeus, *Against the Heresies.*
250. 1 John 2:18
251. Matthew 24:24
252. 1 John 2:22
253. Revelation 13:3
254. Revelation 13:13

a better arrangement of society, that there is no original sin and no Fall. One might go so far as to see a sort of humanist polar reaction to the divine monophysites of medieval times. However, totalitarian regimes belong much more clearly to the realm of the Antichrist. They give absolute power to the state and they mock the Church. Still more, the reign of terror on which they are founded forces everyone to live in a hallucination of lies and deceit, in which even the most simple friendship becomes a source of danger. Finally, for those who have discovered to what extent the Western soul is open to the metaphysics and mind techniques of the non-Christian East, and to those who proclaim a new gnosis (higher knowledge) based on the absolute primacy of the human "I," the apocalyptic warnings of St. John the Baptist and of Christ himself are completely lost.

The enthusiasm of many Christians for "moving with the times"—times, by the way, that leave little room to discover God or one's inner life—ends up by favoring a certain type of superficial Christian militancy, which, paradoxically, leaves the depths of the Western soul open to nostalgia. At the same time the non-Christian East, increasingly in direct confrontation with the Gospel, has lost the relative innocence of its cosmic religion that binds humanity under the covenant of Noah, and is in danger of becoming the tool of the Antichrist.

How vain in the face of this menace are the preoccupations of so many Christians with "building a better world" on this earth. Let them first and foremost be Christians taking their place in the mighty and invisible battle of which human struggles are merely the reflected image. "It is only a cloud: it will pass," said one of the Fathers about a historical cataclysm that had shaken his contemporaries. Not so the army of spiritual warriors fighting the battle of Lent through fasting and prayer; not so the silent duel of the hermit with the devil and with death; not so the ascetic endurance of the hermit drawing all evil spirits to himself so that his brothers should be free; not so those Christians singing their praises out loud in the heart of the fiery furnace of this world; not so the most simple penitential gesture and mumbled prayer: these are what count above all in the gigantic tug of war between this fallen world and the world to come. This is the magnum opus, the great work of our lives, the work of liturgy and of saintliness, by means of which the Church will sing aloud with Michael and all his angels, shattering all the idols, "Who is like God?" "Quis ut Deus?"

This battle is not waged by man alone, but by man's binding himself to Christ through the Holy Spirit. As the Book of Revelation shows there will be no real struggle at the Second Coming. The two beasts will be burned up without being able to resist. The cross is a sign of victory. All those who through the ages glimpsed the fiery end of time under the thrust of eternity have known that "the form of this world is passing away."[255] For them, the message of Revelation merges with the "ascetic memory" of death. This "memory of death" will take on historic and cosmic dimensions. The great works of mankind and earthly objects will no longer count. Political, social, and cultural realities will suddenly fade away. The only way forward will be to commit with one's whole being to the absolute assurance given by the beloved disciple: "the world and its lust are passing away, but he who does the will of God endures forever."[256]

---

255. 1 Corinthians 7:31
256. 1 John 2:17

3.   The Eschatological Character of Church Time

The tension between present time and eternity cannot be resolved
within history but only through eschatology. The end of time has
been in the world since the Incarnation: the final judgment became one with the judgment of the second Adam, who proclaims
that now is the time of judgment, and who is always present in the
"mysteries" of the Church. Breaking through the infernal covering
of this fallen world, the Church is the opening into eternity, made
once and for all by the cross. The cross is henceforth the measure
of justice. Mindful of the final judgment the Church ceaselessly
judges and condemns this world. She calls fallen man to die by the
water of baptism and she calls for the fire of the Second Coming
to destroy the world enslaved to Satan. But this death, in which
we are united with the death of Christ, is in fact a "death of death"
and the judgment is the "judgment of judgments."[257] The Church
is where the person is spiritually reborn with Christ and anointed
with the Holy Spirit. This grants them awareness, beyond death
and judgment, of their own resurrection. "Those who have found
life in Christ in its fullest reality have already experienced the first
resurrection."[258] The first resurrection is that of the soul, which
becomes the conduit of grace to the body and prepares the body
for its second resurrection at the last day. The Christians thus find
themselves both in time and beyond time. The "new birth" shines
an eschatological light onto the present, that reveals all things in
the light of the Kingdom. *Our time is the "end time"* in which the
judgment is carried out in a dynamic manner.[259] This is not some
kind of debased apocalyptic rhetoric. It is a fundamental fact that
time, itself from henceforth eschatological, places us in the presence of the End. The Christ event, through the grace of Pentecost,
belongs neither to the past nor to the future: it imparts its value to
each moment of human history and of our lives.

---

257. Maximus the Confessor, *Quaestiones ad Thalassium*, PG 90.
258. St. Gregory Palamas, 3rd Triade.
259. Translator's note: italics in original.

"Behold, I stand at the door and knock."[260] The Church having breached the wall of time and made an opening into eternity, the God-Man descends unceasingly to consume sin, death, and the tyranny of the devil in the bottomless depths of his divinity. He takes away the anguish of our finite existence that has its roots in the gulf between the created and the uncreated. The Church summons mankind, now delivered from the agonies of the judgment, to attain the land that is beyond judgment. Mankind is called to reach the Ark that victoriously divides the waters of death, to attain the new creation in which mankind can finally live in mutual love and in harmony with the created world, where divine love unceasingly offers us total life. The Church greets each person in the words of St. Seraphim of Sarov: "My Joy, Christ is Risen!" The life-giving spirit makes the miracle of the Resurrection unceasingly present to mankind, in and through the Church, through the sacraments and through holiness of life—which is no less than a person's life become sacrament.

It follows that this is not a static dualism of two eons, of now and of eternity. It is not just the expectation of the Second Coming experienced in linear time and strengthening the memory of the Resurrection. This dualism begins to be resolved in each person, in the holiness of life. This is no less than conscious participation in a lived eschatology, in the deified time of the Church, in which the Second Coming has already begun. For Origen, those who were "perfect" in this world could already enter the world to come[261] through awareness of the profound identity of the second and third Pascha, that is to say, the presence of the Kingdom at the heart of the Church.[262] For in the Church, as in the Kingdom, we have the same High Priest, the same Sacrifice, and the same Victim.[263] As St. Symeon the New Theologian wrote: "The day of the Lord will never come

---

260. Revelation 3:20

261. *Commentary on John*, v.1, PG 14.

262. Translator's note: 1st Pascha = Passover; 2nd Pascha = Death and Resurrection; 3rd Pascha = Parousia.

263. *Commentary on Matthew*, PG 13.

for those who have become the children of light and of the day to come, for they are already with God and in God."[264]

ΩΩΩ

The Christian does not flee from time in search of this sanctification: time is where he serves and bears witness. And so he is strangely torn between the mysterious new creation, in which he participates in divine life, and the fallen world, in which he is wounded, and whose suffering he feels all the more deeply. For the more a person participates in divine life, the more he becomes the bearer of a love that makes him open to the suffering of mankind and to the groaning of the cosmos. And he feels more and more culpable for all the suffering in the world. No doubt it is for this reason that the saints shed so many tears.

But this rending apart of time, even to the gates of hell, is by its very tearing apart an opening onto eternity. Time subject to death is shown to be life resurrected, by the power of the Resurrection. "We the living are handed over to death for Jesus' sake, so that the life of Jesus may also be made manifest in this mortal flesh of ours."[265] The Christian dialectic of time and eternity is resolved in the mystery of the cross, on which death was swallowed up by life. The rending apart of time corresponds to the rending apart of the cross and opens the pathway to the Resurrection. If through the Spirit we can participate in Christ's glorified humanity, let us not forget that this humanity is imprinted with all the moments of the Lord's *kenosis*. These are not so much acts to be imitated as they are deified states, granting the possibility that the most negative aspects of human time can become an opening onto eternity. "If the Lord was crucified, if we truly follow him, we shall also be crucified, albeit on an invisible cross."[266] But, as his

---

264. Lossky, cited from *Homily 57*.
265. 2 Corinthians 4:11
266. Archimandrite Sophrony, *"tiens ton esprit en enfer et ne désespère pas,"* "Messager de l'Exarchat du Patriarche Russe," No. 26.

Transfiguration proves, Jesus tempted, Jesus persecuted, and Jesus crucified was already Jesus deified through his *kenosis*. Since Christ's Ascension, the Spirit grants us to clothe ourselves in Christ's self-abasement through temptation, suffering, and death. And we are given garments bathed in glory and transfigured by eternity. For this reason, "if the Lord was transfigured we will also be transfigured, from this very moment here on earth."[267] This is why Christ said to his disciples, "he who believes in me will (also) do the works that I do, and he will do greater ones than I do."[268] If Christ came to consume all our sufferings, these also become the matrix of his victory. The Lord's death is an inconceivable rending apart: for death can have nothing in common with the deified humanity of the God-Man. On the other hand the death of martyrs is a union of love that delivers them from suffering.[269] After the Resurrection, the Ascension, and Pentecost, it is impossible for man to reproduce the "economy" of the Son. Rather than *imitating* the actions of the incarnate Word, the Christian should be clothed, as he travels through the vicissitudes of fallen time, in those glorified kenotic states, in those epitomes of our fallen nature, that the Ascension introduces into the very heart of the Trinity. One should not therefore say that the Orthodox ignores the *imitation of Christ*: rather that Orthodoxy does not reduce this to an imitation of the tragic humanity of Christ. As regards Christ, this would be a distant echo of Nestorianism and as regards man, this would be a surreptitious and even usurpatious exaltation, as though Christ had not been resurrected. Orthodoxy gives the *imitatio Christi* its full meaning of conformation to the whole Christ, both kenotically abased and glorified, both crucified and resurrected.

We have acquired redemption once and for all: the *imitatio Christi*, which by definition is lived in the light of Pentecost, opens onto the light of Mount Tabor. Pentecost—and the Church

---

267. Ibid.
268. John 14:12
269. "O happy and greatly praised martyrs of the Lord, *suffering with Christ you are consumed by the fiery coals of the Holy Spirit.*" Verses of the Greek Octoikos on the martyrs.

is a perpetual Pentecost—extends to all Christians, without any
limitation other than their personal capacity for faith and love,
the privilege granted for one instant to the three astonished apostles on Mount Tabor. The privilege, that is, of seeing the kenotic
humanity of Christ, "the darkened nature of Adam,"[270] penetrated
and illuminated by glory, *as it was in reality.* "Come let us go up
to the mount of the Lord and to the house of our God, to behold
the glory of His Transfiguration, the glory as of an only Son of
the Father, receiving light from His Light. And ascending by the
Spirit, we praise through the ages the consubstantial Trinity."[271]

The meaning of the "imitation of Christ" lies in theosis, in
the realization of the divine adoption. This takes place not through
a gnostic lifting to the heavens but through conformation to the
divine love of mankind, or "philanthropy." Man follows Christ by
taking up his cross. But whereas Christ died so that his fullness
would take the place of death, the Christian dies to death in order
to receive the fullness of life. The Christian descends into humility: the ascetic "ladders" are in reality descents into humility. At
the limit he becomes pure receptivity, ontological "poverty," and
the prayer for grace: "Lord Jesus Christ, Son of God, have mercy
on me, a sinner." He freely receives the light and the divine life
that the Savior came to give us, the divine light that was and remains the Savior, who is "the way, the truth, and the life."

The Orthodox "imitation of Christ" culminates in the form
of the "poor friend of man" (*ptôchos philanthrôpos*) who claims
no merit in helping others (with only poverty as his being), nor
does he take their place for their benefit (for the One alone made
atonement for all): he claims nothing, he lives in the increasing
certainty of being the "worst of sinners," and he will die, like St.
Silouan of Athos, reproaching himself for his failure to be humble.[272] But unbeknownst to himself, this "pauper" enriches all
men with the "poverty" of the Lord.[273]

---

270. Great Vespers of the Transfiguration, Litia, The Festal Menaion.
271. Ibid.
272. Archimandrite Sophrony, *Starets Silouane*, Paris, 1952. Likewise at his
     death St. Anthony declared that he had not even begun to repent.
273. 2 Corinthians 8:9

"Do not hold me," says the Risen Lord to Mary Magdalene, "since I have not yet gone up to my Father."[274] We now call to the Christ who has returned to his Father. His wounds, the stigmata of fallen time forever imprinted on his eternity, come to us not so much in the blood of those stigmatized on Earth as in the light of those transfigured "paupers."

Here we need to again take up St. Augustine's analysis of time to show that this is only possible from within Christianity.[275] Fallen time is indeed purely transitory, a present that is a moment without substance between the abyss of the future and the abyss of the past, arising from the future only to be swallowed up by the past. Fallen time has no present: it is the expression of an absence—the absence of God, and by extension the absence of man to himself and to his fellow men. By contrast the time of salvation is concentrated in a present born of the presence of God in the heart of our poverty and suffering. In so far as this poverty is no longer a slide into despair but instead, one might say, a slide into divine love, this is a humble opening to the resurrected life of the Lord. "Keep your mind in hell and despair not," said Christ to the Elder Silouan, "for in condemning himself to hell and thus annihilating all passion, man makes his heart free to receive divine Love."[276]

The deified time of the Church both encompasses and exceeds the two conceptions of temporal existence that we have explored. The paradisaical nostalgia of archaic cultures is filled to overflowing by Christ's recapitulation of human history, reopening Paradise to man, the Paradise identified by the Fathers with the Church. But Christ is more than Paradise and so, by consequence, is his Church. The light of the eighth day already shines there. And so our condition is immeasurably superior to that of

274. John 20:17. St. Maximus the Confessor comments, "Let us not restrain the Word forcibly in these lower regions, the Word who of His goodness abased Himself, but let us rise up with Him to the Father" (*Gnostic Centuries*, PG 90).
275. *Commentary on Psalm 101*
276. Archimandrite Sophrony, "Messager de l'Exarchat du Patriarche Russe," No. 26.

Paradise, even while we remain subject in part to the fallen eon. For we no longer risk losing grace: we can always return to the theandric fullness of the Church.[277] Through penitence and faith even the inner core of our fallen nature, which was taken on to its innermost depths by Christ, is opened to the ever-offered forgiveness and to the deifying mystery of love. Meanwhile, liturgical repetition has been transformed from a powerless attempt to return to our origins into an always-renewed encounter, through the natural rhythms with him who ceaselessly comes toward us.

Every Pascha, every Sunday—for Sunday itself is a Pascha—assists us to incorporate sacramental life and therefore to make this encounter ever more intimate. When the water of tears rejoins the life-giving water of baptism, passing through the sands of passion, when, in the words of St. Paul, the person becomes a sanctified host, then their every moment is illuminated by the light of the eighth day, the light of Pascha and of a perpetual feast of Sundays.

Likewise, the linear time of sanctified history is the time of waiting for the Second Coming. This waiting, this vigil, is no longer the future tugging on an empty present. It is the personal ripening of a present so rich that it would crush us, if we were not guided by the Spirit to discover its riches little by little. Time is no longer the domain of faith daring to become hope: time is hope daring, through the grace of the Holy Spirit, to become conscious of love.

---

277. Translator's note: Both of God and of man.

4.　The Jesus Prayer and *Sophrosyne*

The Jesus Prayer saturates human time with eternity, first and foremost, as an internalized Eucharist. As a weapon of penitence, it guards our heart from the passions of fallen time. As a call for help, it turns every life situation into an occasion for humility. As a song of love, it transforms the instant into an encounter with the Beloved. As a summary of Christian faith, it makes our body the receptacle of the Name that sacramentally communicates divine energy. The Jesus Prayer penetrates the fundamental rhythms of lived time: breathing and heartbeat. Through the Jesus Prayer temporal existence becomes a celebration of eternity, even while we sleep, revealing the rhythms of the body to be symbolic receptacles of divine grace, the human breath of the divine spirit.

"He who acquires the Spirit and is purified by the Spirit breathes divine life."[278] Those who have in this way "raised their spirit to God and established their soul in God's love have transformed their flesh, which shares in the ascent of the spirit and joins in the divine communion. Their flesh becomes the habitation and house of God."[279] After "burning tears have poured abundantly from the heart, cleansing bodily, psychological and spiritual pride,"[280] they are bathed in the light of the eighth day, in the glory of the Resurrection. Eternity is revealed, not as an abstraction, not as something that has an independent existence, but as God himself in his essence, in the pouring forth of divine energy.

Mystical rapture and ecstasy are only steps along the way. Far from fleeing time, the saint takes part in a *personal, deified temporal existence*, in which the holding back of grace plays the essential role in the long period of instruction in the divine. The saint internalizes the deified time of the Church, receiving each instant from the hand of God with complete trust. The saint does not claim to have consumed time, in the manner of the Hindu who has achieved deliverance. Nor does he claim supernatural

---

278. St. Gregory of Sinai, *Petite Philocalie*, p. 248.
279. St. Gregory Palamas, *Petite Philocalie*, p. 232.
280. Archimandrite Sophrony, "Messager de l'Exarchat Russe," No. 14.

powers. For the saint, time becomes the "synergy" of freedom and grace, and the "apostolic" love of one's neighbor. To claim a share of eternity while still on earth would, in a way, be to treat God as an object. But to remain in time while realizing that nothing belongs to man by right is to accept total dispossession and to expect nothing, except that it comes from God, placing oneself entirely in the hands of an Other. The saint does not have the power of spiritual discernment, if this is understood as something that can be acquired. But he knows how to achieve total inner silence, the silence of "pure prayer," and the first thought born of this silence comes from God and is the word of discernment. "The human soul is open to you and you can read it like a book," said a visitor to Seraphim of Sarov. "Oh no, oh no," the saint replied humbly, "the human heart is open only to God, for it is a bottomless abyss. . . . I say to those who come only what God commands me to say. I consider the first phrase that comes to me to be a message from God. But if I have to find the answer myself, I am easily mistaken." And he added, "I have placed my will in the hands of God as the iron is placed in the forge, and I only speak when I sense that the word has been given to me."[281]

This is the essence of saintly time: a "spiritual sabbath" in which man discovers matter aflame even within the confines of daily life—a silence of adoration in which the Spirit gives birth to the Word, for the salvation of one's neighbor.

ΩΩΩ

If there is a spiritual quality that Orthodox asceticism attaches to the eschatological character of the present, this may best be called *sophrosyne*—which can be defined approximately as "chastity" or "integrity."

In its most immediate sense *sophrosyne* denotes the eschatological mystery of virginity. St. Gregory of Nyssa tells us that

---

281. V. Zander, *St. Seraphim of Sarov*, p. 25 (French ed.).

fallen time is "soiled" because it has been subject to many generations and cycles of corruption. The "flow" of time (*rhysis*) is soiled (*rhypôsa*).[282] In destroying the eros of Paradise,[283] sin has replaced "the impulse for life" of primitive time with the "impulse for death" of sexuality. Or more precisely, the tragic conflation of these two impulses has given rise to the negative aspect of cyclical time, in which burgeoning life gives rise only to death, in a cycle without end. But since the Incarnation and Pentecost we stand in the "dawn" of the eighth day, of that unique day that, with the Second Coming, will bring once and for all the "pure impulse for life" of the longing for divine union.[284] Even while on earth we can free ourselves from the dirty floodwaters of time through the ascetic and spiritual protection of virginity, and partially anticipate the world to come. This virginity, it should be understood, is conceived of not as mere continence, but as the rediscovered integrity of the whole person,[285] who is already a participant in the economy of eternal life.[286] St. John Climacus writes: "Those who, being clothed in mortal flesh, have received the gift of chastity for their labors, have died and have been completely reborn. They have tasted the first fruits of the incorruptibility to come."[287] It follows that spiritual virginity is essentially eschatological: it makes present the world to come, in which we will be like God's angels, who do not marry.[288] By chastity we are reborn into eternity and stand beyond the voided span of human generations. "Through their first birth of flesh and blood, men arrive on earth and disappear just as rapidly. There is a second birth of spiritual purity that occurs when the light descends on those who have been washed by the waters of baptism. Our third birth purifies the obscured

---

282. St. Gregory of Nyssa, *De Octava*, PG 44.
283. According to St. Gregory, man would have multiplied in Paradise in the manner of the angels.
284. *Épectase.*
285. Translator's note: this meaning of *sôphrosyne* is captured by the Russian *tselomudrost'*.
286. See especially St. Gregory of Nyssa, *De Virginitate*, PG 46 and *The Creation of Man*, SC 6.
287. St. John Climacus, The Ladder, 15th Degree, *On Virginity*.
288. Mark 12:25

image of God in us, through tears and suffering. The first of these births is from our mother and father. The second is from God. But in the third birth we become our own father, appearing to the world as a light of good deeds."[289]

To turn eros inward is to prevent eros from engendering life and death. With respect to time, this is to wrap it in itself in order to burn up time in the fire of the Spirit, in the unveiling of the time to come—in brief, this is to hasten the Second Coming. Preferring heavenly reality to its time-bound image, the virgin celebrates the true bridal feast, that of Christ and his Church, of the Word and the Christian soul.

But the Church also holds that marriage can be a state of chastity that witnesses to the end. In making clear the analogy between the Christian couple and the union of Christ and the Church, and by extension their participation in this union, St. Paul situates marriage in an eschatological perspective. The apostle and Christ himself emphasize that "the couple has its origin before the fall. Through their union the Christian couple rejoins the first creation, the New Adam, of whom they become the forerunners."[290] As two persons who are of one nature, the Christian couple forms "a little church," which, as St. John Chrysostom writes, witnesses by its constitution to the "catholic" mystery of the Trinity.[291]

With the announcement of the End we arrive at full personhood. In these "last times" marriage no longer has the purely functional goal that it had before the Incarnation, when, fulfilling the divine promise, generation followed generation. Now it achieves its full meaning as personal communion, as the union of man and woman in one body and one soul, but in two persons, to use the formula of Balsamon, the Byzantine canonist.[292]

289. St. Gregory Nazianzus, PG 37.
290. J.J. Von Allmen, *Maris et Femmes d'après saint Paul*, 1931, p. 36.
291. St. John Chrysostom, PG 62. In marriage the form of the sacramental is conjugal love: "marriage is the sacrament of love," St. John Chrysostom, PG 51. See also Paul Evdokimov's important study "The Sacrament of Love," which takes this for its title.
292. Cited by P. Evdokimov.

Likewise, childbearing is an arrival into full personhood. According to St. Paul "the woman is saved through motherhood."[293] It would be a mistake to interpret this statement in the light of the Old Testament view of barrenness: a childless couple reaches fulfillment in proportion to the love that they radiate.[294] What the apostle seems to be saying is that even the most fallen reality, the "death impulse" that arises from the dirty floodwaters of generations of corruption, is saved and transformed into a sacrament of the world to come. For the deeply personal, that is essentially Christian, takes priority over all functional over-estimation of procreation. The "joy that a human being has been born into the world"[295] is the wonder that is felt in the face of the absolute newness of each person, before this face that is called to become an icon, before this being whom God loves, and who is in some way essential to accomplishing the fullness of deified humanity.

Therefore, if the chaste ascetic burns up duration, the Christian couple transforms the nature of time. If the chaste ascetic denounces the world as null and void, the couple traces out the metamorphosis of creation. There is no contradiction here, only a complementary relationship in which virginity, on the higher rung, shoots for the goal from the outset, while Christian marriage strives to illuminate the path. We might say that the transfiguring light of marriage finds its source in virginity. "Christian virginity reaches to the end of the arc, whereas marriage is a stop along the way. Virginity takes its place in the line of the *great sacrament* whose earthly state it transcends. Virginity directly attains the very essence of the heavenly wedding feast, the metaphor used by so many of the Fathers for the Church and Christ. Virginity becomes a discourse on the theology of espousal to Christ the Word."[296] Rooted in spiritual virginity, chastity

293. 1 Timothy 2:15
294. The recurring appeal of *syneisaktism*, or spiritual marriage, in which a couple violently refuses sexuality, proves by its excesses that the Christians of the first centuries indeed understood marriage in this personal and spiritual perspective.
295. John 16:21
296. Dom Olivier Rousseau, *Monachisme et Vie Religieuse*, Chevetogne, 1957.

appears as a transfiguring force destined to penetrate all aspects of life, in order to integrate them into eternity. Virginity is the salt in every human undertaking, by means of which Christians preserve the world from decay and transform it into an offering acceptable to God.[297] Virginity denotes the dynamism of the person who is able to free himself from his nature, in order that it may receive grace. A marriage is chaste when it is not simply dissolution of the person into instinct and passion, but instead tenderness surpassing and personalizing the flesh, transforming it into the sacrament of encounter. Water is turned into wine at the wedding at Cana: from the eucharistic perspective this can be understood as the transfiguration of eros, a transfiguration that is at the root of the universal transfiguration. Chastity introduces us to the third aspect of the time of the Church, that is, the construction of the Kingdom of God.

---

297. Cf. the symbolism of salt in Leviticus 2:13. See also Appendix 1.

5. On Certain Limits of History

The Kingdom of God is not built through the collective works of human history, nor is it built up through the work of the Church, through "doctrinal development" or otherwise. The Kingdom is built in time, at the level of the person, but for eternity.

The mission of the Church is to communicate the Good News to humanity, to people, not to the collective forces of history. In the Christian vision of history, the Church must boldly be what Hegel called the corner store of faith. Christians must calmly accept that they are treated as "simple souls," since for them real history is what transpires in the depths of each individual's existence, and only subsequently in the clash of empires, ideologies, and "the masses." Indeed, real history has its locus in the infinitude of inner space, in the spaciousness of the human heart, in that mysterious encounter between each human destiny and God. This can only be known by the two participants, and, sometimes, by those whom the Holy Spirit joins to the ways of God.[298] In the words of Origen to the Savior, "as for me, I do not wish to be seen by anyone except You alone, I wish to know by which path I may reach You, and that this shall remain secret between us, that no-one shall act as intermediary, that no passing stranger shall witness."[299] Each person's acceptance or refusal of God is the beginning and end of all human history.

For personal salvation is also the salvation of humanity: far from being a self-serving evasion, personal salvation is achieved through openness to all of life, through the struggle for the communion of mankind. When St. Polycarp was arrested and martyred, on the supreme occasion of his personal encounter with God, he requested his captors to allow him an hour for prayer. This was not so he could plead for his "individual salvation" but so he could remember "everyone, whom chance had ever brought him into contact with—great or small, known or unknown, as

---

298. The *cor spatiosum* of St. Augustine.

299. Origen, *Song of Songs*, quoted by Urs von Balthasar, *Origen: Spirit and Fire: A Thematic Anthology.*

well as the entire world-wide Catholic Church."[300] The very notion of "individual salvation" is a contradiction in terms. To be
saved is to escape from the fragmentation of individual existence,
in order to make real the unity of humanity that was restored by
Christ, a making-real accomplished in the life of the person who,
mirroring the life of the Trinity, is open to all other persons, that
is to say, who is in communion—sacramental communion being
the root of communion with other people.

What can we know of these simple mysteries? One person imagines that he is worshiping God, when he knows God
only as a concept; another knows the love of God, yet appears
indifferent; another worships him through blasphemy. Is there an
atheist who has not anxiously drawn in his breath on an evening
of desolation, as if in the obverse of a prayer? What "observant"
worshiper has not suddenly seen that his God is no more than
a comfortable habit, his Church a refuge from life, its routines a
soothing rhythm? These questions are not posed as part of a liter-
ary game or as an invitation to relativism. I want only to suggest
that real history is the history of love, and that human love only
achieves its fullness when it is open to the divine love from which
it receives its strength. And this can only be within the bosom of
the Church. True history culminates in that saved and conscious
love that is saintliness. While those who do not join themselves to
Christ are scattered, those who make even the least gesture in the
name of the Lord have more impact on the destiny of the world
than any assembly or army. The saints are the true masters of the
world: it cannot be overstated how many times the destiny of the
world has hung on the prayers of an unknown saint. The true
historical actors are to be found among those whom superficial
history ignores or distrusts—among the outcasts, émigrés, prisoners, and the sick, those "failures," those "little people" whose
very existence is an offense to the idolatry of wealth. If these turn
toward God, they do so with their hearts opened by their experience of "historical defeat" and by the teaching of the divine school
of suffering. Likewise, the women and children, whose humble

---

300. *Martyrdom of Polycarp, Early Christian Writings.*

secrets of "private life," filled with the sense of mystery, are more valuable than any collective raptures. These innumerable "suffering servants" make up, as it were, the reserve of love from which the martyrs arise, because God makes his strength shine through our weakness. Among them, we should not fail to include the truly creative, for whom the demands of a higher love and nostalgia for eternity collide with the objective historical reality.[301]

The events of visible history are therefore the result of the deification of the created world, which is being prepared within the Church. The multiple intersections of humanity and human destiny converge in deification: "known only by God and by those to whom the Holy Spirit has revealed them. This is the book of life, sealed with seven seals, that St. John was granted to read, that will not be opened to us until the Day of Judgment."[302] This is not to say that the work of the historian is in vain, but it should resist global explanations and grand systems that comfortably bind together the superficial facts of history, while vainly or proudly ignoring grace and freedom. The Christian historian refuses to reduce the person to a cog in an unfolding present, or to reduce freedom to the act of awareness of historical inevitability. This history can never be completely intelligible, as it remains wordless about the hidden depths of human and divine freedom. It must examine all points of view in all honesty, each shedding light on the other, without claiming to reduce everything to one theory that reigns over all others. This history emphasizes the complexities of the unfolding present, and the limits of all preliminary explanations.

In recognizing the complexity of human reality and the limitations of historical understanding, the historian begins to approach the depths of human experience and to grasp the different existential levels on which a person may be placed with regard to the current moment. In summary, this history respects choices freely made. History that respects real experience demands an

---

301. Citing a theme dear to Berdiaev.
302. Vladimir Lossky, *Cours de Théologie Dogmatique*, unpublished. Subsequently published as *Dogmatic Theology*, SVS Press: Crestwood, NY.

apophatic understanding of man: it becomes an analysis of the circumstances under which freedom is exercised, rather than an analysis of *causes* claimed to determine the scope of freedom. As a phenomenology of the temporal and societal nature of man and of the psycho-social conditioning of mankind, this history leaves intact the transcendence of the individual over his situation. While a person can never escape their current situation, they can choose how to view it, and the situation itself changes according to how it is seen.

They can become completely wrapped up in the situation, adding weight to its negativity and destructiveness. Such passive complicity is one of the forms of enslavement to sin. Or they can decode the troubles that assail them as the language used by God to invite their repentance and their love, at this precise moment in time, in this precise place. In that single movement they open themselves to grace and freedom, breaching the opaque sinfulness of the unfolding present, and allowing the fire of the Spirit to enter into history, strengthening the seeds of life.

In this way, authentic history leads beyond the exploration of "natural conditions" to the discovery of personal freedom and to the *encounter with the other*. Therefore a Christian history, no matter how scrupulous its erudition, will not be fruitful, unless it also opens itself up to the domain of freedom and grace, transforming the phenomenology of the epoch into an ascetic path of opening and welcome. Its mission is to prepare us for the human encounter with those whose love has penetrated their time, and who have inscribed it into eternity for us, their brothers and sisters. In this way history leads us beyond tombs and ashes to the kingdom of the living where it is rooted in and transformed by the communion of the saints.

To complete this necessary cautionary note against the idolatries of the present, we must examine the ostensibly negative aspects of Christian attitudes toward politics, that is, history in the making.

A Christian lives like a stranger in his own country, devoting himself to serving the common good, while being aware that social and cosmic order depend, in reality, on his prayer. According to the Epistle to Diognetus, "Christians live each in their own country as if they were resident aliens. They carry out all their duties as citizens and accept all the burdens as though they were strangers. They are at home in every foreign country and every country is foreign to them. They pass their life on earth but they are citizens of heaven. They obey the established laws but in their manner of living they exemplify a perfection beyond these laws."[303] It is not that they are unaware that the realm of Caesar and the realm of God will both endure until the Second Coming. However, they proclaim Christ alone as Lord. This testimony radically changes the perspective of all human endeavor. Christ, not Caesar, is the Kyrios, the Lord of history. At the same time, the Church prays for those who govern, those who judge, those who bear arms, even if they are overtly atheist. In this way the Church consecrates the mystery of the legitimacy of secular powers, as was clearly stated both by Jesus Christ and by St. Paul. This in no way signifies that the Church imposes its conditions on secular power; rather that the Church proclaims Christ as the Lord, not Caesar. The legitimacy of secular power means that the Church hierarchy may not claim secular supremacy or call for rebellion. For the Orthodox, the possibility that the pope could call on his subjects to break their oath of loyalty, the theory of the two swords, the Jesuit apology for tyrannicide, and the continued maintenance of the secular power of the papacy, even if in a mostly symbolic form, are all symptoms of a fundamental error. Only the suffering of the confessors and the blood of martyrs can bear witness, at one and the same time, to the reign of Christ and to the legitimacy of human power. The Christian bears witness that Christ is the Lord and delivers his life voluntarily for punishment, declaring himself guilty of having disobeyed the earthly powers that are God-given, even when idolatrous. The Orthodox Church has adopted this position without exception, toward pagan Rome, iconoclastic emperors, Islam, the eighteenth century "enlightenment" of Catherine the Great, and, finally, toward communist rule.

---

303. SC 33

This double act of witness forms the basis of the Christian civic attitude: the Christian must obey Christ and Caesar at the same time, owing his conscience to the first and his life to the second. This "at the same time" cannot be other than a cross.

For the Christian, the only legitimate reason for war is the defense of contingent realities, recognized as such: the land, the hearth, the country. This sacrifice, stripped of any hatred of the enemy, is an act of love that belongs with commitment to the absolute truth. Spontaneously-offered blood consecrates the soil and strengthens the mutual love of those who inhabit it. The conscious gift of life, to protect a reality that is loved even in its transience, conveys the fullest value to personhood, while sanctifying and even externalizing this reality. But the Christian must reject all exaltation of the partial, any enshrinement of concept, any submission to ideology and to verbal idols. Furthermore, the Christian should refuse to fight for any absolute truths, for only divine love is absolute. The "wars of religion" were not Christian: nor is a war undertaken in the name of religion. The Church lives in the presence of him who stayed Peter's sword in the Garden of Olives.

At the limit, Christianity implies nonviolence, bearing witness to love alone, even to the point of humiliation and martyrdom. This should, incontestably, be the position of the monk and the ordained minister. A long-forgotten ecumenical canon calls for defrocking a deacon, priest, or bishop who, when attacked, resists with force. The lay member of the royal priesthood should choose, depending on his personal circumstances, between Christian nonviolence and the attitude of the "holy prince," who gave his life to defend the future of those whose care was confided in him. To decree a norm would be fanaticism. The only command is self-sacrifice.

6.   Dogmatic Development and Tradition

Although the history of the Church unfolds in secret in the communion of the saints, out of sight of the historian, should one
nevertheless not admit that there is "progress" in the knowledge
of the truth, and that there is a "development" intrinsic to the
growth of the rule of faith and to the ever "richer" interpretation of dogmatic thinking? There is a widespread belief in such a
collective unfolding of revealed truth over the course of the era
of evangelization, notably in the Roman Catholic Church. Sometimes this takes the form simply of an intellectual ambiance, such
as that which led Père von Balthazar to call the patristic writings
"this private diary written by the Church when it was seventeen
years old."[304] (We should not allow ourselves the facile sarcasm
of asking to what extent the Church of today exhibits signs of
senility.) Sometimes we are confronted by an elaborate system in
which the soul takes the role of the mythological unfolding present, such as the Christian evolutionism of Teilhard de Chardin.
This, one should note, is outside of the official teachings of the
Church. Above all, ever since Newman, the most serious Catholic
theology has given an increasingly important place to the idea of
dogmatic development.[305]

From this perspective, the dogmas of the Church are to be
found in the two sources of revelation, Scripture and Tradition,
but some are "explicit" and others are "implicit." The transition
from "implicit revelation" to "explicit revelation" constitutes dogmatic development. A truth defined by the Church would have
been previously "implicitly revealed" when "the revelation is sup-
ported neither by sufficiently clear scriptural or traditional doc-
uments nor by common and universal established practice."[306] In
this case, dogmatic development may be taken to represent the
intellectual awareness of a truth that for a long time had remained

---

304. *Présence et Pensée*, Paris, 1942.
305. Translator's note: Cardinal Newman, the nineteenth century Anglican di-
      vine who became a leading Catholic thinker and cardinal.
306. *Dictionnaire de Théologie Catholique*, "Dogme."

nascent and imperceptible, whose formulation required a real process of maturing. And so, while Bossuet denied papal infallibility and Thomas Aquinas denied the Immaculate Conception, we are nonetheless told that these doctors of the Church were not heretics. In their time, we are told, the dogma that they rejected had not yet reached maturity and therefore they could not yet grasp it.

For the Orthodox such a theory is scarcely permissible. It would imply an organic development and a vitalistic and ultimately unconscious conception of knowledge; that seems to me to be hardly compatible with the constant presence of the light of the Holy Spirit. For those Catholic theologians who are closest to the Orthodox conception, Pères de Grandmaison, Lebreton, and de Lubac, dogmatic progress occurs in the transition from one state of knowledge to another, from a pre-conceptual, unformulated, and visceral knowledge to an abstract, conceptual, and fully formulated knowledge. But how can we label as knowledge something that the conscience of the Church did not just ignore, but formally denied for centuries? Such is the case with the nineteenth century dogmas that can only be justified through the theory of dogmatic development.

We would have to abandon the Orthodox conception of Tradition, guarded by Christian people as a whole and by the communion of saints, one in time as in space, and then invoke the action of organic upheavals of which we were long unaware, whose truths, out of reach of the catholic conscience of the faithful, are warranted at the time of their emergence by a superior, infallible authority, that is to some extent exterior to the Body of Christ in which the Spirit resides. It is in fact significant that the theory of papal infallibility was defined at the same time as the theory of dogmatic development. Something that was held to be an error in the twelfth and thirteenth centuries became a truth in the nineteenth century. This would indicate that the vital movement of knowledge is reduced to unawareness, pure and simple. From another perspective, the idea that transition to an abstract and conceptual state of knowledge constitutes progress would appear to us to imply far too great a confidence in the power of reason. Such confidence could never be allowed by the Orthodox apophatic conception of dogma. Now, says St. Paul, we know "in part," which is to say that, beyond any human faculty of knowing, we personally cleave, with all our being, to the presence of God, which is not yet "all in all." We know "in part" because our knowledge opens onto a fullness that cannot be grasped conceptually. Dogma, as partial knowledge, preserves our access to this fullness. And only the Parousia, not dogmatic development, can overcome this limitation. Dogma is necessarily a partial expression of the revealed mystery, which it stakes out, opening concepts to the heavens and humbling reason through negation and antimony. Within the idea of dogmatic development lurks the temptation of rationalism—the illusion that doctrine can explain the mystery. But any doctrine "that claims the fullness of knowledge is in reality contrary to the fullness in which we know things in part."[307] Orthodoxy rejects the idea of a *dynamic state* of knowledge, which in fact leads to ignorance and makes universal truth time-bound. Orthodoxy also rejects any claim to explain the fullness of the mystery rationally, as it is beyond the play of conceptual definition. Orthodoxy places the emphasis on personal and existential knowledge, grounded in faith, knowledge which in our earthly existence is always only partially articulated through human expression, but which opens onto the fullness of the Holy Spirit. Since the first Pentecost the Holy Spirit has offered the illumination of each individual conscience. This growth in awareness occurs at the level of each individual person, rather than in the collective unfolding of humankind.

Some Necessary Comments on the Orthodox Conception of Tradition and Dogma

For the Fathers, Tradition is not another pathway of revelation, running in parallel to the Scriptures. Tradition is the Church itself carrying forward, through its whole life, what St. Irenaeus called

---

307. Translator's note: quoted without citation in original.

the Hypothesis of the Scriptures.[308] Here we should understand
hypothesis in its strict etymological sense to mean "that which lies
beneath" the Scriptures, that is to say, their meaning and their
unity, the breath that enlivens them and makes the words of Scripture "the unique body of Truth." *Paradosis*, that is, Tradition, is
the life of the Holy Spirit in the Church. It is the communication
of the Spirit through which the Christian deciphers the portrait
of the Lord in the "mosaic" of the Scriptures: it is the presence of
Christ that explains all of the Bible and that now pronounces the
Word in the Church. Without this unifying Spirit, we would have
nothing more than colored stones arbitrarily arranged by individual whim—like the madman who from a mosaic of the emperor
composed the portrait of a dog.[309]

The apostles gave us the body of scriptural revelation,
and since that time the Spirit that inspired them has helped the
Church to guard their message, and to adapt it to each epoch
through preaching, teaching, meditation on the Fathers, and iconography. Tradition is therefore the unique mode through which
revelation is received, as Vladimir Lossky stressed.[310] Tradition is
not the substance of revelation; it sheds light on that which has
become apparent. "For the God who said: 'out of the darkness
light shall shine,' has made a light in our hearts for the radiance of
the knowledge of the glory of God in the face of Christ."[311] "See to
it that there shall be no one to steal you away by philosophy and
by empty deception according to the tradition of men, according
to the fundamentals of the world, and not according to Christ."[312]

Tradition is the communication of Truth by the Spirit, that
enables us to know the Truth in its own light and not in the exterior and completely human light of fallen reason. Tradition is not
the Word itself, but is the breath that carries the Word and grants
us to understand the Word as the Word of God. That is to say, it is

---

308. *Against the Heresies*
309. Ibid.
310. Introduction to V. Lossky and L. Ouspensky, *The Meaning of Icons*.
311. 2 Corinthians 4:6
312. Colossians 2:8

the breath that grants us to encounter the *incarnate* Word and to understand it in its relation to the Father. Through the Word, and through all the expressions of revelation that the Church offers us through its "mysteries," Tradition reveals the silent presence of the Father to us. St. Ignatius called it the "Word of His own from silence proceeding"[313] and said that he "who has truly mastered the utterances of Jesus will also be able to apprehend His silence."[314] This is perhaps the best definition of Tradition.[315]

ΩΩΩ

Tradition is life-giving. It conserves while being renewed, bringing a message to the people that speaks to them in the language of their existence and of their suffering.

This renewal in no way implies conceptual elaboration. The Truth cannot consist of an ever-evolving set of concepts in an evolving system. The Truth is wholly present in each stage of human history, and the Church in its wisdom makes the Truth manifest, in the manner that best corresponds to the problems and errors of the moment. Rather than indicating a sort of organic growth, the history of dogma reveals the conscious response of the Church to the historical context in which it is called to bear witness. "The Old Testament clearly revealed the Father, but only indirectly revealed the Son. The New Testament reveals the Son but only suggests the divinity of the Holy Spirit. Now the Spirit is among us and reveals Himself in all His splendor. It would not have been prudent to openly preach the divinity of the Son before the divinity of the Father had been openly recognized. And as long as the Son had not been accepted, it would have been imprudent to impose the Holy Spirit, if I can dare speak in this way."[316]

---

313. Epistle to the Magnesians 8:2, *Early Christian Writings*, p. 73.
314. Epistle to the Ephesians 15:2, *Early Christian Writings*, p. 65.
315. "the Kingdom of God is not in speech but in power to act" (1 Corinthians 4:20)
316. St. Gregory Nazianzus, PG 36.

To use this quotation from St. Gregory in support of dogmatic development is to ignore the fact that ever since Pentecost "the Spirit dwells with you and will be in you."[317] St. Gregory wants to show that, in the *economia* which it presents to the world, the Church should imitate the divine pedagogy of the Lord in times past. Guided by the Gospel antinomy that there is "nothing secret that shall not be revealed,"[318] but that pearls should not be thrown to swine,[319] the Church "does not reveal all at once, without discrimination, and yet does not keep anything hidden until the end. The first would be imprudent; the second would be impious. The one risks wounding those who are outside the Church: the other risks driving away those who are our brothers and sisters."[320] Dogmatic definition is therefore affirmed in response to history, actualizing the knowledge of the Truth through the fire of the Holy Spirit. This permits the Church to discern true from false, and to "re-situate" its teaching, the kerygma, with respect to the unfolding of the human spirit, keeping open the narrow door through which the intellect, crucified and illuminated by faith, gains access to the fullness of Truth. Dogma, as St. John Cassian wrote with regard to the Antiochian Creed, constitutes "a précis of the words of the Lord, compressing the faith of His two covenants into a few words, so as to contain, in brief, the full sense of the Scriptures."[321] Instead of dogmatic "evolution," we should speak rather of "involution." The fullness, the all-in-all, that is always present in the Church contracts in order to respond to the difficulties of the moment and becomes distilled in a dogma that bounds, protects, and points forward to the mystery. There can be no rest in the struggle for the salvation of the world. We cannot be content with simply repeating Scripture or with simply repeating the theological formulas of the past. We must always seek to express the Truth anew. We must transmit the *hypothe-*

317. John 14:16
318. Matthew 10:26; Luke 12:2
319. Matthew 7:6
320. St. Gregory Nazianzus, PG 36.
321. John Cassian, *De Incarnatione*, PL 50.

sis to people in their language, transforming Scripture into living word, spoken today by the Lord in the Church that is his Body, and illuminated *today* by the fire of Pentecost.

ΩΩΩ

To understand the nature of a collective unfolding of history you only have to observe the attitude of the world in permanent confrontation with the Church. Here there would seem to be an obvious evolution, as the choice between the two ways of the psalmist, between Christ and the lie, is posed ever more categorically. The development of the "noosphere"—the realm of abstract knowledge—closed to the transcendental and anchored in the technological power of humanity, initially in the technology of matter and now in the technology of mind, with its resulting dehumanization and *decosmication*: these are just aspects of the person stripped bare and, through anguish and boredom, thrown ever further into the fundamental dereliction of the void whence they came, and to which they will return, whose painfully tender personhood nevertheless testifies that they were created in the image of God. Beyond the world of daily atrocities and forced happiness, beyond the ultimate idolatry of the ascetic pursuit of self, the direction of this evolution is without doubt toward an ever more lucid awareness of hell, a "flight from the face of God" that draws closer to Christ, because the Christian message is that Christ has conquered hell and death.

No one would deny that there is an evolution in collective consciousness, attuned according to the epoch to one or another aspect of the Christian message. But the Church can only respond to this evolution by witnessing to the immutable. Theology casts chasm-defying "devil's bridges" between the immutable and the evolving world. In their victory over error these open onto a vision of the all-in-all.

This correspondence between the unfolding world (to which Christians are present) and the fullness of *Paradosis* does not occur automatically. The Spirit does not act through some infallible agent but through the Church as a whole, on which it has descended. That is to say it acts through the individual consciences of those whose detachment, humility, and love have made them guardians of the Truth. Individual consciousness can only grasp the fullness and define the Truth through a long creative effort. For the sixty years that separated the two great ecumenical councils, all the genius and strength of the great Cappodocians was needed to preserve the mystery of the Trinity from the opposing Sabellian and Arian heresies. This takes us to the core of the Christian dialogue with Tradition: the Church has always baptized "in the name of the Father, and the Son, and the Holy Spirit," as the Lord instructed. And even though they did not know the term itself, St. John and St. Paul had as acute an awareness of the Trinity as the Fathers of the fourth century.

But major currents of human thought attempted to *explain* the living God and to dissect the fullness of personal being. Arianism was steeped in the thought of Aristotle. Thesis and antithesis are counterposed as in Hegel's dialectic. On one side, the unity of God was emphasized to the point of swallowing up the Persons of the Trinity. On the other side, the sharp distinction made between the Father and the Son shattered the Trinity and made the Logos merely the first created being. However, the dogma that protected and revealed the mystery of the Trinity was neither a mere synthesis of opposing heresies nor an exercise in rational explanation. From the opposing heresies it defined an antimony in which the two terms *ousia* and *hypostasis*, essence and person, transcribed the grandeur of the Trinitarian doxology into the heart of dogma: "Glory to the Father and to the Son and to the Holy Spirit."

Once achieved, such dogmatic definitions never become obsolete. The errors that they define are perpetual sources of attraction to human nature, the "natural" declivities of human reason. At the same time, dogmatic definitions provide an opening to the fullness that guides our faith. The ways of approaching the Truth are constantly adapted throughout history, but always in line with the proven continuity of its ancient forms of expression. In clarifying a "new" dogma, the Church always takes the already defined body of dogma as its starting point. This is not an "enhancement" of Tradition, but rather a conscious "economy" inspired by Tradition. The Fathers of the Seventh Ecumenical Council rightly distinguished between "the authority of our holy Fathers"—the horizontal dimension, or "economy" of the construction of dogma—and "Tradition," which transmits inspiration on the vertical axis, "because we know that Tradition is the voice of the Holy Spirit that dwells in the Church."[322] St. Paul speaks of the growth of the Body of Christ as a "building."[323] The growth of the rule of faith is the result not of an organic thrust forward, but of lucid elaboration, inspired by the Spirit. The "building" of the Body of Christ is in this way comparable to an inspired composition, to a work of art.

ΩΩΩ

We are now in a position to understand how there are distinct periods in the history of the Church, in which the accent is placed on one or another aspect of Revelation. Schematically, we may say that Orthodox thought has passed through three major phases, that are each imbued with the sense of totality (because they are inspired by one and the same fullness). The succession of these phases corresponds to the articles of the creed, on which they may be seen as a commentary, according to the demands of history.

For the first eight centuries, theological attention was clearly fixed on the first two articles of the creed, which proclaim God as Creator and Savior, and Christ in his double relationship with God and humanity. We can call this the Christological period. It culminates in the Chalcedonian Symbol of Faith, or Creed, and bears its final fruit in the declarations of the Seventh Ecumenical

---

322. Denzinger, *Enchiridion Symbolorum*, no. 302.
323. Ephesians 4:12

Council on the veneration of images. But we already see the third
Person of the Trinity coming into focus. The icon shows the human person becoming holy to the extent that it can take on the
deified humanity of the Savior. If the Christological period above
all emphasized the first rock of belief—"God became man"—the
working of the Incarnation shifted the center of gravity of the
meditations of the Church to the corollary "God became man so
that man could become God."

During the ninth century, the Orthodox Church defended the second part of the creed, which concerns the Holy Spirit and its "economy," initially in the sanctification of the person,
and then in the whole life of the Church. This decisive change
in theological "economy" passed mostly unnoticed by Western
Christians. The Western schism occurred just at the beginning of
the new period, and the teaching on the Holy Spirit was precisely
what was at issue. From this point on, Western religious thought
remained, despite its enormous energy, trapped in archaic "ho-
moiousian" modes of thought, which were unilaterally developed
in the confines of the doctrinal elaboration of the *filioque*.[324]

By contrast it was in the Christian East, so frequently denounced by Western historians as "fossilized," that the Church
experienced the true era of the Holy Spirit. It is however true
that the mysteries of the Holy Spirit do not give rise to the same
solemn and fully elaborated doctrinal definitions as the Christological debates. Without making too much of the play on words,
one might say that the doctrine of the Logos, the Word, is more
naturally expressed through the mode of logic, whereas the grace
of the Holy Spirit embodies hidden dynamism, life, and inspiration, that open onto a fullness that cannot be expressed in words.
God reveals himself in the Word, but the Spirit plumbs the silent
depths of divinity. The shape of life in the Church also changed
strangely in conformity with doctrinal shifts. The Christological definitions resounded in the city and throughout the unified
world of the Roman Empire. By contrast, the Byzantine Empire

---

324. Translator's note: *homoiousios*, meaning of a similar substance/essence; as
opposed to *homoousios*, meaning of the same substance/essence.

contracted step by step, while whole new peoples became Christian. That unity which seemed to speak of the economy of Christ was succeeded by an effervescent, diverse medley of Church life that is a metaphor for the mysterious action of the Holy Spirit.[325] The Roman Church, trapped in a unilateral Christological framework, artificially maintained unity through a Latin liturgy that was incomprehensible to its people, while the Eastern Church translated the Scriptures and the liturgy into the languages of the newly converted peoples, most notably the Slavs.

The great teachers of the period of the Holy Spirit were first and foremost contemplatives who expressed themselves in poetic language. St. Symeon the New Theologian sang hymns both to the Holy Spirit and to the personal encounter with Jesus in the light of the Holy Spirit. This is another confirmation that the whole truth is always present and that there is nothing one-sided in St. Symeon's emphasis on sanctification by the Holy Spirit. Nor was intellectual rigor lacking. The thirteenth and fourteenth centuries were the time of the great doctors of uncreated grace: Gregory of Sinai, Philotheus of Constantinople, and above all, St. Gregory Palamas. But in distinction to Western scholasticism, these teachers rejected any notion of "natural theology." "Deconceptualizing" earth-bound theological concepts apophatically, they opened them up vertically, making them instruments, albeit partial and incomplete, of a fullness that both transcends and illumines.

In this period there were also councils which, without being declared ecumenical, obtained the consent of the entire Orthodox Church. The Council of 879 rejected the *filioque* and at the same time St. Photius clarified that the person of the Holy Spirit proceeds from the Father, the one and only source of the divine, and is revealed by the Son. In this way the Church defended the integrity of the Person of the Spirit, as well as the Spirit's "economy" in the world. From this perspective the Incarnation

---

325. Consider the extreme diversity of iconographic styles in Bulgaria, Serbia, Georgia, and Russia, and the various provinces of the Byzantine Empire itself. Consider also the richness of musical styles, in which domain Bulgaria played a major role.

is ordained at Pentecost: Christ came to prepare the medium—his own body—within which the Spirit could descend in order to "deify" humanity. God took on a human body so that man could take on a spiritual body.[326]

The era of the Holy Spirit reached its apogee in the fourteenth century, when the Constantinople Councils of 1341 and 1351 gave their assent to St. Gregory Palamas's distinction between the essence and the energies of God. God is "completely other" and radically intangible in his personal transcendence, but by grace we can receive his uncreated energy, his life itself. We can look upon the light of the Transfiguration with our own eyes.

By degrees, thinking on the Holy Spirit turned its attention to the Church itself, so that, without disappearing completely, the "pneumatological" period transitioned into the "ecclesiastical" period. Theoleptus of Philadelphia and St. Gregory Palamas emphasized that the experience of divine love—as hymned by St. Symeon—is none other than the personal coming to awareness of the inner mysteries of the Church by the grace of the Holy Spirit. The light of Tabor flows from the eucharistic host. In the same period, Nicolas Cabasilas and Simon of Thessalonica revealed the spiritual profundity of the liturgy and the great richness of the "great sacraments of initiation."

In the same period, St. Nicodemus the Hagiorite edited the Philokalia, a true summation of contemplative life, and St. Seraphim of Sarov and the Russian *startsii* of the nineteenth century spread the practice of the Jesus Prayer from the inner walls of the monastery to the Christian laity. This was a response to the rational and technical optimism of contemporary thought, just as Palamism was the Church's response to the naturalism that was growing in the heart of Eastern and Western religious thought. The Philokalia and St. Seraphim's transfiguration prove that the Church is not an end in itself: it is wholly oriented to the free sanctification of mankind.

Nonetheless, the dominant emphasis of theological thought is on the Church. The Grand Council of Moscow of 1666-67 re-

---

326. St. Athanasius, *On the Incarnation*, PG 26.

jected all ecclesiastical monophysitism by emphasizing the "synergy" of two wills in the life of the Church: the will of God and the will of man, the synergy of us and the Holy Spirit. The Council of Jerusalem of 1672 took up the same theme, addressing the sacraments and defending the sacramental "mystery" of the Church from both the "automatism" of Rome and the Calvinists' radical distinction between the visible and invisible. This council emphasized the role of the *epiclesis*, the prayer for the descent of the Holy Spirit, in all of the mysteries and sacraments of the Church, and above all in the Eucharist. Here God, by his own will freely sending the Holy Spirit to change the bread and the wine, encounters the will of man, in the form of the outpouring of the prayer of the epiclesis, in which the Church asks for the descent of the Holy Spirit, so that the glory of the eucharistic presence may become manifest.

In the nineteenth and twentieth centuries, the nature of the Church itself becomes the focus, thanks to an increasingly close dialogue between the Orthodox and the other Christian confessions, a dialogue aided by the political events of the twentieth century and by the ensuing Orthodox diaspora.

In 1848, the Encyclical of the Eastern Patriarchs stressed that Tradition is preserved by Christian people as a whole, by the communion of "catholic" consciences, which is the image of the Trinity. In 1872, the Council of Constantinople resisted the surrender of the Church to nationalism and ethnic passions. The territorial principle corresponds to the sanctification of the world by the Church: the Church should salt the creative work of mankind with the savor of eternity, while rejecting the Babel of separatism. The local church, gathered around its bishop, the guardian of the integrity of the preached word and of the eucharistic transformation, in communion with all the other churches, constitutes the Church as a whole.

In the twentieth century, the sophiological controversy placed into question the relationship of the Church to society and to the cosmos. In the message of the imprisoned bishops of Solovki and that of the future patriarch Sergius in 1927 there are strong echoes of the Epistle to Diognetus.[327] The whole context of our time places the Church in question: the social question, the unification of the planet, the cosmic responsibility of mankind, the correlative nostalgia for a retreat into self—in brief the demands and the idols of our time. Perhaps more than other Christian communities Orthodoxy can emphasize both the ontological unity of humanity, which was assumed by Christ, and the uniqueness of each human person anointed by the Holy Spirit. Perhaps only the Orthodox Church offers a cosmic vision of the Church. From another viewpoint, the deepening of hesychastic practice and the practice of the Jesus Prayer (in the Roman Catholic Church, for example) lays the foundation for a response to the rapidly growing new gnosticism, gnosticism fuelled by the rebound of non-Christian Eastern religions.

Will Orthodoxy, with its sense of the end times and its spiritual depth, have the opportunity to bring all its human and cosmic import to the understanding of the doctrines of the Church? This is the new battleground.

---

327. *Early Christian Writings*

7.   Building the Kingdom of God

If a person comes to Christ not just passively accepting the Truth, but bearing stones or better still themselves becoming a stone in the building of the tower that Hermas describes, then they come with their whole being, with all their personal experience and with all their historical and cosmic specificity.[328] Personhood is neither a closed self-oriented individualism nor a disembodied spirituality. A person takes on the full depths of their being, in order to open these depths to grace. Thus they acknowledge their duty of care for the earth and for humanity, and first and foremost for their land and their people. The children of the Church are also children of the earth, formed from its flesh, fed by its harvest, and welcomed back into its peace after their death.

The earth and human communities become part of human nature. A person must embrace them in order to reach his full stature. In saying this, we must reject any communal perspective: a person is not a cell or social organism, or the mere instrument of the soul of a people or the destiny of a land. Notions such as these lead rapidly to idolatry. The people and the land are relative, time-bound realities: only the person is summoned to an absolute goal. A person is not saved by the mediation of nature or of history: instead nature and history are saved and freed by the person who makes them participants in the work of Christ. Nonetheless, the soul of the land and its people is real, existing not as an organic entity but as a personal encounter and as an always-evolving outline of common creation, of true communication. Formed from the coalescence of personal freedom, fed by works of collective creation, tarnished by bloodshed and war, a nation's historic destiny is a divine calling revealed by its guardian angel, and molded into recognition by the tears and blood of the saints and martyrs who have made flower the desert of soil and human hearts.

328. The Shepherd of Hermas, Vision III.

In living out the liturgy a person strives to sanctify all the works of the world. By the grace of the Spirit, we build on the foundation that has been laid, namely, Jesus Christ: "the fire will prove the nature of each man's work" consuming the "hay" and the "straw" but transfiguring the "gold, silver and precious stones."[329] The royal priesthood of the Christian encompasses all aspects of civilization and all the beings of the universe, "even the serpents," according to St. Isaac the Syrian. Consecrated by the Spirit, the Christian becomes the secret king who brings peace to his own nature and thereby to the universe. He is the priest transforming the ambiguous beauty and lamentation of the earth into hymns of praise. Christ, the recapitulation of the universe, grants man to gather the *logoi* of beings and things, and to decode them and to offer them back to God in their full original meaning, as revealed in the glorified Body of Christ.[330] Finally, the Christian is the prophet who, denouncing the idols and announcing that the Kingdom of God is at hand, enters its hidden presence and hastens its arrival.

The Church is the woman in childbirth of the Apocalypse who cries out in pain in giving birth to the new man, and through him, to the world that is to come. Time and eternity descending as a newborn child, the celestial Jerusalem comes "out of heaven from God, wearing the glory of God."[331] The saint sees this descent into the depths of matter, and brings it to be. The universe only reaches its full dimension in the vision of man: this is why a saint is transformed by prayer and love. If we fail to see the light that glows beneath the mortal shell, we have only our own blindness to blame. The Second Coming, the Parousia, will only explode into our world when all of the "chosen people" have "enhypostasized" the universe, have transformed the universe into the Trinity, each in their own way, revealing it to be the glorified

---

329. 1 Corinthians 3:11-13

330. *Logoi*: this expression, Stoic in origin, took on a biblical meaning, especially with Maximus the Confessor, for whom *logoi* designates things in their created reality, words contained within the Word made understandable by the Incarnation.

331. Revelation 21:10-11

Body of Christ. *Maranatha*: saintliness is the "let it be," the *fiat* of the Parousia.

In ongoing fallen time, the royal priesthood wages a peaceful battle that regulates and protects the cosmic order and human society.[332] The benedictions of the liturgy are in reality "benefactions," to use the expression of A. Frank-Duquesne, that ensure the fruitfulness and fecundity of cyclical time, and are given additional force by personal prayer.[333] We pray for "favorable weather" and the "abundance of the fruits of the earth" and in so doing we shield innumerable lives from decomposition and chaos.

The building of a church, the installation of a cross, the presence of icons in the home, all these serve to exorcise the cosmic powers, to facilitate human relations and, in a completely real way, to modify our whole milieu. Through their labor that is "salted" with prayer, Christians roll back the borders of the spiritual desert and make peaceful landscapes bloom, in which the garden of Paradise finds its reflection. Outside of Christ, man places his creations in a cosmic dimension: his temple is a cosmic mountain; his garden is a return to the beginning of time. Only the Christian peoples, each according to their particular gifts, give the earth a human face, so that, no longer bound in idolatry, it can turn toward God. The re-creation effected by Christ enables man to become a true creator: under the inspiration of the Holy Spirit, he reveals the creative power of God at work in matter and nature, participates in them, and "gives birth" to the beauty with which this matter is pregnant.[334] The collaboration of man and God makes the high creations of art holy: they wrench man from his monadic subjectivity and reveal God's creation to him. In iconography art becomes consciously liturgical. If what is falsely called profane art can become a feast in Paradise, what is rightly called sacred art is an eschatological prophecy. For this reason the saintly task of iconography is fully equal to the saintly works of the monks.

---

332. Matthew 5:13, "You are the salt of the earth." See also Appendix I.

333. *Cosmos et Gloire*, Paris, 1947.

334. The image of pregnancy, which occurs frequently in the Scriptures, is applied by St. Paul to the cosmos (Romans 8:22).

Cosmic maternity is sanctified by authentic human creation, by the blessing of a meal, of work, of the harvest, and finally and most importantly by the eucharistic transformation. As we see in the Book of Revelation, the earth comes to the rescue of the Church. "But the snake cast from his mouth behind the woman water like a river, so that he might have her swept away on the river. But the earth helped the woman, and earth opened her mouth and drank down the river which the dragon had cast out of his mouth."[335] Cursed because of Adam's sin and Abel's blood, the earth offered a cave to Mary and a tomb to Christ. The same earth that formed the glorious Body was purified by the blood of the Lamb, and was exalted in the Ascension. As the bodies of the saints return to their earth, the earth becomes as it were the sole body of humanity, and as such it is bound for resurrection. Thus the earth has formed an alliance with the Church and wants to become Church, and in a strange way offers protection to Christians.

Even in silence, the presence of a saint casts a shadow of peace on the earth, like a long undervalued and mutilated tree whose still presence we today recognize. "To put it briefly, the relation of Christians to the world is that of a soul to the body. As the soul is diffused through every part of the body, so are the Christians throughout the world . . . the soul, shut up within the body, nevertheless holds the body together, and though they are confined within the world as in a dungeon, it is Christians who hold the world together."[336]

$$\Omega\Omega\Omega$$

And so, by force of their prayer, through their act of being present and then through their participation in creation, the Christians fight to transform the earth into sacrament and to transform culture into an icon of the heavenly Jerusalem, into

---

335. Revelation 12:15-16
336. *Epistle to Diognetus, Early Christian Writings*, p. 145.

which the nations shall bring their glory and honor.[337] History tells us that this is always a work in progress, never completed, the fruits of which will only be seen at the Second Coming. This work leads to sainthood, and sainthood, so long as it is not universal, is painful. To sanctify oneself is to discover that communion is the very structure of personhood. It is to pray that the holiness of him who alone is holy illuminates all mankind and through mankind the entire universe. While the saints after their death rest on the Sabbath day, this rest is expectation.[338] Christ himself, according to Origen, awaits the full glory of his heavenly Body, in an incomplete state.[339] "For there is only one body that awaits perfect blessedness."

The heavenly expectation of the saints is transformed into collaboration with Christians on earth for the building of the Kingdom. This is the image of the unity of the Temple of the Apocalypse, at once of the world and not of the world, anchored in Christ by the great free exchange of love, and by the relationships that are woven without ceasing between humanity on earth and humanity in heaven. The communion of the saints builds the Kingdom. Saintliness eats away at worldly totalitarianism. In the Middle Ages it was thought that the great monastics were the avenging angels of the Apocalypse. History is crisscrossed by lightning and supra-political signs. Thus Christian antiquity celebrated Constantine's military standard, with its *Chi Rho*, and the death of the Emperor Julian, whose dying words were "Galilean, you have conquered." There continue to be signs and wonders. After the Bolsheviks blew up the Cathedral of the Holy Savior in Moscow in 1937, the soil refused to bear the weight of the monumental tower that they wished to build to the glory of communism. And again in Russia, in the heart of the great persecution of the Church, icons became as new in front of thousands of witnesses and the sun lit up the domes of the churches.

---

337. Revelation 21:26

338. Revelation 14:13, "they may rest from their labors, for what they have done goes with them."

339. Origen, *On Leviticus*, Homily 7.

The Christian constructs eternity in the light of these signs, while accepting incomprehension, failure, and martyrdom in diurnal time. "Blessed are the peacemakers, for they shall be called the sons of God." And the Son of God was crucified. In holy Russia, it was believed that the tsar should die a martyr, giving his life for his people, as did Christ. This is also the obligation of each faithful Christian as they exercise their royal priesthood. When there is no longer a political expression of royalty, in a society become hostile or indifferent, the function of royalty continues to be expressed in the prayers and service of each Christian. In the Book of Revelation we see the role of the Christian king give way to the reign of the saints.[340] This is for our times an early and precious indication of the end of the Constantinian "symphony" of Church and state that we are now experiencing.

When Christians give their life, day by day or in a single act, they should know that, through all their earthly failures, they are reconstructing the world in the mode of eternity. Like the "passage of a poet," their work, bathed in prayer and love, offers God's creation up to God and offers man up to God and to God's creation.[341]

ΩΩΩ

And therefore, carrying the name of Jesus in their hearts, Christians must take part in the common work of humanity, to use an expression of Fedorov's, without spiritual fear or earthly vainglory, storing up treasures in the eternal storehouse that is the Church.[342] It is the Christian's task to bring the best of all the lands, of all peoples, and of all cultures, into the true Ark. Christians should take part in science, technology, art, and political life with no other purpose than to be Christian. That is to say, they

---

340. See Revelation chapters 20-22.
341. Referencing the novel of the same title by Ramuz. See Appendix II.
342. N.F. Fedorov, *Filosofia obshchevo dela*. See biographical note in A. Schmemann, *Ultimate Questions*, SVS Press, 1973.

should fight to transform the relation of man to man into communion, and the relation of man and earth into transfiguration.

Fedorov wrote that our social program is the teaching of the Trinity: anything that strays from this preordained plan is no more than a sociological heresy. Clericalism—the imposition of the Church on politics—is a degenerate and partisan version of Christianity that is no longer an expression of the universal faith but instead seeks to impose the truth from outside, by the threat of execution. By contrast, the Christians who discover themselves to be a conscious member of the "little flock" should work from the inside, through the unseen powers, that is to say through penitence and prayer, and through love, love that has an infinite respect for personal freedom and that sacrificially takes on the life of all matter and all beings. It is pointless to fight for a "Christian civilization"—these are merely the garments of the Church, the garment that Christ let the soldiers divide beneath the cross. We do not fight, politically, in the name of Jesus, but instead with the tools of this world, for the social and political forms through which the fervor of the Christian people was once expressed. But we awaken a creative faith in ourselves and around us, so that when he wills God will again clothe the world in a Christian culture. Unless, that is, in these times of accelerating apocalyptic intensity, God wills his Church to be stripped more bare, to become more like the Crucified One, her arms open wide to all of life, to all humanity, preparing for the definitive arrival of the Kingdom.

"Find inner peace and the multitudes will be saved alongside you," said St. Seraphim of Sarov.[343] This was his reply to the question of whether it was better to stay in the world or to retreat from it. The era of Christianity's grandeur has ended, in which too often the Church intermixed with "the world," without truly making it Christian. The Christian must now be both of the world and apart from it. "I do not ask you to take them from the world but to keep them from evil. They are not of the world, as I am not of the world . . . As You sent me into the world, so I sent them

---

343. Translator's note: quoted without citation in original.

into the world."[344] In the depths of the nineteenth century, the Virgin of La Salette spoke of the "apostles of these latter times," who, according to St. Thérèse of Lisieux, would sit at the sinners' table. At the same time, the elders of Optina caused monasticism to explode into the life of the Russian laity. Dostoevsky, unlike Dante, finds Christ in the depths of that modern hell which he explores and shows us the elder Zosima sending his disciple into the world.

To speak symbolically, one could propose that the conscious Christian should today fulfill two roles, that of monk and that of king, the two poles of the *laos* of God in the old Christian society.

Interior life can no longer be the realm of the specialist, while each person must assume their responsibility for history and the universe. Too often this sense of responsibility places Christians at the beck and call of "this world." But we forget that our responsibility is not measured according to the criteria of this world, but according to Christ's commandments. His first commandment is to love God with all your heart and with all your mind. A contemporary monk of Mt. Athos wrote that hesychasm, that goal of which is to place the one who prays into a state of "pure prayer," is simply the strict application of this commandment.[345] The inverse of this is surely the diffuse heresy of the modern world, which prioritizes the second commandment, to love one's neighbor, to the point of completely forgetting the first.

ΩΩΩ

All political battles are children's games, a surface iridescence, by comparison to the eternal battle of the Gospel. The ways of God are not those of men: and only those filled with the Holy Spirit can know them, or rather can lose themselves in them. The

---

344. John 17:15-18
345. Archimandrite Sophrony, *Des Fondements de l'Ascèse Orthodoxe*, Paris, 1954.

way of the saints is often a shock to the wisdom of the historian. St. Geneviève repelled the Huns but allowed the Franks to conquer Gaul. St. Gregory Palamas and other most authentic spokespersons for Orthodoxy in the fourteenth and fifteenth centuries accepted the rule of the Turks. God guides those who pray in his ways, not those who agitate. To take another example from the early history of France, the Merovingian era would seem to present only sterile barbarism. But if we pay closer spiritual attention, we will see the struggles of the saints who were building the soul of France itself, building up reserves of strength that would feed the French nation for centuries. True creative acts are first and foremost spiritual, and they can only flourish in the hidden fullness of the Church.

Is it too simplistic to note that earthly cities perish, menaced as they are by sclerosis or by revolutionary chaos? Only the Church, which is in the world without being part of the world, has an uninterrupted and continually creative tradition. To make one's mark on the perishable earthly city it is necessary to draw deeply from the eternal youthfulness of Tradition, that is, the youthfulness of eternity. Christians are aware that earthly values are relative, and for that reason they can be made use of without fear of idolatry. To know that everything must die and therefore that everything must be saved is to love with a true love. To sacrifice oneself for a reality that one knows is relative is the only way to endow that reality with eternal value.

In face of the precarious beauty of culture and the earth, the Christian attitude should be that of the ascetic who, seeing a beautiful lady by accident, "began to praise and glorify the supreme beauty of which she was the creation, and thereby felt himself transported by the fire of divine love, melting into a stream of tears. If someone like this great man in this and in similar encounters receives such feelings from God, they should be considered as one of those who, while still living in their corruptible body, have been resurrected into an incorruptible body, even before the general resurrection of the dead."

We should strive to be filled with the same urge to praise God when we hear music: "for when they hear a beautiful harmony those who love God are moved by holy joy, by divine affection, and by a tenderness that brings them to tears, be it a popular song or a spiritual anthem."[346]

This should be how the Christian is present to the works of civilization: to welcome them, while exorcising them; to baptize them, putting an end to idolatrous self-sufficiency, in order to give them life in the light of the Kingdom; to be part of the relativity of time in order to bring eternity. The Christian fights to transform every situation and every reality into a prophecy of the Kingdom that already participates in the world to come. And when the "prince of this world" attempts to turn the life of this world into a closed system, the Christian proves by his martyrdom that Jesus is the only Lord of history. As a sacrifice of intercession for all, including the executioners, martyrdom witnesses to the fact that the wall of separation has forever been abolished. "A Russian bishop, cruelly tortured to death during the revolution, said that his torturers' only hope on the Day of Judgment would be the pleading of the Martyr, who alone has the right to pardon them in the name and image of Christ."[347]

---

346. St. John Climacus, *The Ladder*, 15th Degree, *On Chastity*.
347. Unpublished letter of an Orthodox bishop, dated August 1957.

8.   On Hell

"Keep your mind in hell and despair not."[348]

The Orthodox Church places no limits on the freedom of God or of the person. And therefore it places no limits on the loving-kindness of God, nor on the possibility of a person's eternal refusal of this loving-kindness. The Orthodox Church declares that there is a "natural" apocatastasis that is not personal.[349] At the Second Coming, God will be altogether in us, the uncreated light will transform the universe, and human nature will be healed and illuminated: or rather, the whole of life will make manifest the glorious Body of the resurrected Christ.

God can only give his love. But those who, closed in on themselves, cannot freely accept this divine love on the day of judgment, will experience God's love as unbearable fire. The uncreated light is total awareness. What can hell be if not the impingement of this awareness on the vertiginous subjectivity of non-being? Hell is not eternity: it is non-existence that refuses eternity. "It is not correct to say that sinners in hell are deprived of the love of God . . . But love acts in two different ways. To the outcasts it becomes suffering and to the blessed it becomes joy."[350]

ΩΩΩ

Nevertheless, the real theological problem (taking theology in its highest sense of the knowledge of spiritual life) is not so much hell as the right to speak of hell.

---

348. Christ's words to Silouan of Athos
349. The expression *apocatastasis panton*, used in Acts 3:21, signifies the universal restoration, the re-establishment of all things in God.
350. St. Isaac the Syrian, *Spiritual Homilies XI*, PG 34.

Can one dare to speak of hell for other people? Is this not to offend against love and thus to condemn oneself?

Only God has the right to speak to *me* of hell. The Gospel parables on the sheep and the goats are addressed to me. They warn me and call me to repentance.

There are some subjects on which one cannot speak calmly. Speech must yield to prayer.

I cannot speak of hell except for myself: I am the "worst of sinners"; how will I escape from the eternal regret of spurned love? But the greater my fear, the greater my hope. Christ has conquered hell. I cannot escape from his love unless by taking refuge in my selfhood. And fear itself cracks open selfhood, opening my personal hell to the prayer of the thief: "remember me O Lord, in Thy Kingdom."[351]

"When Thou comest, O God, upon the earth with glory, the whole world will tremble. The river of fire will bring men before Thy judgment seat, the books will be opened and the secrets disclosed. Then deliver me from the unquenchable fire, and count me worthy to stand on Thy right hand, Judge most righteous."[352]

But the Judge is also the Defender. "A handful of salt in the immensity of the sea, thus are the sins of all flesh in comparison to the loving-kindness of God,"[353] says St. Isaac the Syrian. For him, the real sin is to not pay enough attention to the Resurrection, which was made ours by baptism. What counts more than fear is repentance in faith, constant faithful attention, the attentiveness of one's whole being to the "joy of the love of Christ: how can Gehenna stand when faced with the grace of his Resurrection?"[354]

ΩΩΩ

---

351. From the Orthodox prayers before communion. See also Luke 23:42.
352. Kontakion for the Sunday of Last Judgment, Lenten Triodion.
353. St. Isaac the Syrian, Sentences CVII.
354. Ibid., Sentences CXVIII.

As for other people, I can pray only that they may be saved. No one is alone. In Christ we are all members of each other, of one Body. The others are in us and we are in them. The love of God, multiplied by the prayers of mankind, works from the innermost part of the ultimate hell, the monadic individual, to explode the monad into the divine unity of the Kingdom.

In the Orthodox prayers for the dead, it is never implied that some are already eternally damned. Wholly focused on the Second Coming, the Orthodox Church does not make the Latin Church's distinction between hell and purgatory. The Orthodox pray for all the dead. This prayer takes on a special solemnity in the kneeling prayers of the Sunday of Pentecost. "Deign to accept our petitions for those imprisoned in hell, thus giving us great hope, and relief to the departed from their grievous distress and Your comfort . . . And place their spirits where the Righteous dwell, counting them worthy of peace and repose; for the dead do not praise You, Lord, nor do those in hell dare to offer You glory, but it is we the living who bless and entreat You and offer You propitiatory prayers and sacrifices for their souls."[355]

ΩΩΩ

The Church confesses the natural restoration of all things and prays for a personal restoration. If God does not promise this to us, it is also because he is, in a certain way, waiting for our love.

St. Isaac the Syrian prayed "even for the demons."[356] St. Paul wrote, "we will judge the angels."[357]

Christ descended into hell to destroy hell. This is also inscribed into eternity as the very mystery of the world to come. This is what the Church proclaims and what she forever offers to humanity:

---

355. Kneeling Prayers of Pentecost, 3rd Prayer, Greek Orthodox Archdiocese of America.

356. St. Isaac the Syrian, Sentence XV.

357. 1 Corinthians 6:3

"Let no-one weep for his iniquities, for pardon has shone forth from the grave . . . by descending into hell, he made hell captive. He embittered it when it tasted of His flesh. And Isaiah, foretelling this, did cry: Hell, said he, was embittered, when it encountered Thee in the lower regions. It was embittered, for it was abolished. It was embittered, for it was mocked . . . O Death, where is thy sting? O Hell, where is thy victory? Christ is risen, and life reigns . . . To Him be glory and dominion unto ages of ages. Amen."[358]

The Church is the young woman with blond hair seen in a vision by Hermas, the new tree born from the original rock.[359] *The Church does not evolve: it transforms all evolution into the Word that will accomplish its task in silence. The sacrament of the world to come, the Church proclaims that the Kingdom is at hand, and with the cross, her only sword, she kills in order to bring life. The chain of saints, the force of their transfiguration, corrodes the reign of death in order that love can appear: love that is not solely immobile in time or dynamic in eternity, but is the Ineffable, the Unity in Trinity, that reveals itself as love.*

The Church prays with the Didache:"Let grace come and let this present world pass away."[360] *She gives her full eschatological force to the prayer that the Lord teaches us without ceasing, the prayer that brings us to the "sanctification of the Name"—(that is to say to martyrdom)—the prayer that tears us away from the temptations of these last times; the prayer that from the humble bread of the Lamb pours forth lightning and the cross, anger and love, the anger of love, the judgment judged aright, humanity deified, the transfigured universe.*

"Thy Kingdom Come"

---

358. The Pascal Homily attributed to St. John Chrysostom, The Paschal Service, Orthodox Church in America.
359. The Shepherd of Hermas, Vision III.
360. *Early Christian Writings*, p. 195.

Appendix I

Author's note to footnotes 297 and 332

"You are the salt of the earth."

"You shall season all your cereal offerings with salt; you shall not let the salt of the covenant with your God be lacking from your cereal offerings: with all your offerings you shall offer salt."[361]

The idea that Christians are "the salt of the Earth" and the "light of the world" has a cosmic dimension. On the one hand the presence of Christians in the world prevents its decay; on the other hand they give the world an aroma, a direction, that transforms the world into offering and prepares its transfiguration. The oldest of the apologetic writings, those of Aristides, states: "I have no doubt that it is because of the intercession of Christians that the world exists. . . . They devote their lives to such prayers."[362]

This doctrine is profoundly rooted in the Old Testament: the Christians are the just who were spared at Sodom.[363] The same doctrine is found in the Talmud, in which the world is preserved thanks to the intercession of the thirty-six just men of Israel, who are renewed from generation to generation, and who "daily receive the Shekhina," the presence of God. In the fourth century, Serapion of Thmuis, the friend of St. Athanasius, wrote to the solitary hermits of Egypt: "the universe is saved by your prayers; thanks to your supplications, the rain descends on the earth, the earth becomes verdant, the trees bear fruit, and each year, the floodwaters of the Nile irrigate all of Egypt."[364]

We find a similar doctrine in Shiite Islam, as Louis Massignon has noted, that of the saints whose apotropaic prayer and hidden suffering preserve the universe and hold back the hand of destiny.

---

361. Leviticus 2:13
362. Aristides, *Apology*, XVI.
363. Genesis 18:24-32
364. *Epistle ad Monachos*, PG 40.

Appendix II

Author's note to footnote 341

Passage of a Poet is a novel by Charles Ferdinand Ramuz (Swiss novelist, 1878-1947), in which Besson, a basket maker, arrives at an inopportune moment in a wine-growing village in the Vaudois, in Switzerland. They need buckets, not baskets. In the six months after the time of his arrival, from the first buds of spring to the harvest, he reorganizes the village and renews its life, arriving at the seventh month of peace and joy. When he arrived, the region was ruled by sickness, hatred, isolation, poverty, the impossibility of attaining love, and finally death. But Besson, the poet, is there, and his presence alone, so different and yet so near, resets the whole human condition. His systematic refusal to be anywhere other than among the people whom he is with, or to be anything other than fully himself, brings an end to the world he found on his arrival. This world is reborn to a future of health, reconciliation, communion, generosity, love, and life. This story, as the author perhaps was aware, sets out the task of the Church in the world.